Out of the Silence

Also by Ralph Butler

MY SON

RALPH BUTLER

◆

Out of the Silence

WITH A FOREWORD BY
C. EDGAR WILKINSON
M.SC., D.D.

THE R̶E̶S̶E̶A̶R̶C̶H̶ P̶U̶B̶L̶I̶S̶H̶I̶N̶G̶ C̶O̶M̶P̶A̶N̶Y̶

the Attic Press, Inc.
GREENWOOD, S. C.

© RALPH BUTLER, 1978
ISBN 0 7050 0059 1 (paperback)
Printed in Gt. Britain for The Research Publishing Company
(Fudge & Co., Ltd.), London.

Contents

FOREWORD

by Rev. Dr. C. EDGAR WILKINSON

The Rev'd. Ralph W. Butler, whom I have known for many years, has written a very thought-provoking book which I am happy to recommend. In *Out of the Silence* he brings under the microscope many kaleidoscopic reflections of religious experience: repentance, faith, righteousness, prayer, healing, peace, as well as the life and teaching, death and resurrection of Jesus. As he states, his purpose is to set the reader thinking, with a view to a better understanding of life, a clearer understanding of your relationship to God, and the peace, joy and power that these bring! This close examination, he makes plain, 'is the product not merely of the writer's personal thinking and conclusions, but of a small group of Christians who thought it worthwhile to get together to share a common concern for others; remained together to share the real joys of fellowship and love, and in so doing these things found at last a way to share with God'.

At the heart of the book there is much about the place and power of thought in human life. This is a very relevant reminder for, as Dr. Charles Brown, an American preacher, wrote in his book on homiletics, 'it is not modern thought of which I am afraid; it is modern lack of thought'. Mr. Butler's freshness of approach is most commendable whether one agrees or not with everything he has to say. And if thinking leads to understanding, and understanding to action, and action, through the development of character, to destiny, this book could do a world of good.

1

By Way of Explanation

In writing this book I am not trying to sell you a new idea. Nor do I claim to have found the final answer to many questions that are being asked by people the world over. It is no part of my intention to convert the reader to some new cult, nor to push the claims of any particular religious sect or denomination.

I hope that you will have the interest and the patience to read to the end, and if by that time you have been led to think more often and more deeply of spiritual matters, or to give more time to meditation and communion with God, I shall have been sufficiently rewarded.

A few years ago a group of thinking Christians in America met together to discuss a question which has been troubling most sections of the Church for many years "*What has gone wrong with the Church?*"

It was inevitable that their thoughts should turn to the circumstances in which the "Church" first came into being nearly two thousand years ago. In common with many other seekers after the truth, they decided that the Church was born on the day of Pentecost following the Ascension. In fact they felt that the Church really came into being when the earliest followers of Jesus "*received power from on high*".

There was some justification for that if only because it marked the earliest recorded attempt by the disciples to "preach" what has come to be known as "The Gospel of Jesus Christ". Thus it was natural to give a good deal of thought to the question of what is meant by receiving "Power from on High".

In the first century a person was considered to be "converted" when he or she accepted Jesus as Lord and Master, and publicly declared the fact by being "baptised". But this was only a beginning — not an end in itself. The next step was for such a person to "receive the Holy Spirit" (whatever that meant). This happy state did not, except in very rare instances, follow instantly or automatically. It came as a result of "waiting upon God". There was a period of preparation, prayer, expectancy, patience and *Constant Communion*.

Convinced that the secret of the Church's early *power* lay here, the small group of seekers decided to put their belief to the test. They formed a "Circle of Prayer" with very strict rules. Only *True Seekers* were admitted. Every member must be prepared to give a certain amount of time each week *without fail* (there could be no excuses for absence except in cases of severe illness). Punctuality was important. At a given time the door of the meeting place was locked and latecomers would not be admitted.

Their meetings began with "the breaking of the bread" (the Sacrament of the Lord's Supper reduced to complete simplicity). They continued with a reading of Scripture followed by silent prayer — *long periods of prayer*. From time to time people in desperate need or sickness were mentioned by name so that prayer could be united and directed, but few words were spoken and most of the time was spent in complete silence as the group *waited upon God*. They waited for and *expected* a "Pentecostal" experience.

This experience did not come at once, but the expectancy increased with every meeting. The first tangible result of this experiment was the birth of a deep love for each other in what had begun as an ill-assorted group having only one common interest — the search for *truth*.

Details of the intimate experiences of this group as they continued their work are not available. One aspect alone concerns the writer at this moment — the "movement" (if it may be so termed) "caught on" and within a few months many other such "circles" were formed in different parts of America, and within a year several such groups had formed in other countries the world over. The writer, in fact, became the leader of such a "circle of prayer", and this book was born out of his experiences in that capacity.

Such prayer circles are essentially *non-denominational* in character though they may well be born within any Church of any denomination. They have this special characteristic: *they are not just another organisation or function* of the Church in which they are born. *They do not grow in numbers*. The membership of a single circle remains constant (never exceeding twelve) until such time as one or other of the members feels "prompted" and "qualified" to begin a *new circle*.

The question may well be asked: "Is this not the beginning of still one more division within the Church? Is this not exactly how new "sects" come into being?" The answer is definitely *no*. And the reasons are quite simple.

1. Each circle is restricted in size, twelve members being considered an absolute maximum.
2. There is no liaison between different circles nor is such a thing desired or encouraged.
3. There are no rules, regulations or laws beyond attendance and punctuality. The *Law of Love* operates as a "result", not a condition.
4. Members of the circle usually become better members of their own Churches, and because of the non-denominational character of the circle, more tolerant of other Churches.

The circles accept and are guided by one basic truth, that "where two or three are gathered together in His Name — there is Christ in the midst".

This book is not an advertisement. It is not an appeal. It is not even propaganda. It is written only because unmistakable prompting was received during meetings of the circle of which the writer was a member. Though it will give you much food for thought, above all things *it is not to be considered as a text book.* Jesus Himself never wrote such a book and none other has the right. God deals with individual souls, not with masses.

It is the earnest prayer of the writer that this book may lead you to a better understanding of life, a clearer understanding of your relationship to God, and the peace, joy, and *power* that these things may bring into your life.

If we, as a circle, in our human weakness, have misread certain signs or misunderstood the promptings we have been given, so that what is here written might tend to mislead you, we pray that our efforts may be *overruled* by the Holy Spirit.

This book is intended to do no more than to set you thinking — seeking — hoping — and expecting.

2

Communication

In these modern days the Church is often blamed because it does not keep abreast of the times. Young ministers, particularly, stress the point that the Church continues to speak in an archaic language which is no longer understood by, nor acceptable to, the youth of today. The accusation is just and reasonable in spite of the fact that the grandeur and beauty of the Bible language has no equal in the world, but the remedy applied is very often quite futile.

To modernise a language needs more than the substitution of "you" for "thee" and "your" for "thy". It is not enough to say "hit" instead of "smite" and "truly" instead of "verily". What is needed is to *understand* the language, and to convey its message in terms which mean the same today as they meant two thousand years ago.

There are still, unfortunately, tens of thousands of people, spread over the world, who regard the Bible in its "authorised" version almost as if it were written by the very hand of God. Any alteration of the text is regarded almost as heresy. No attention is paid to the difficulties which faced the early translators, nor will it be accepted that errors inevitably crept into the text. It is difficult to persuade such people that modern science and twentieth century thinking is not aimed at discrediting the Bible, but at making it clearer and more understandable.

This chapter, however, is concerned with only one of the words which is used unchanged today after thousands of years. It is a word used more often, perhaps, than any other by religious people, and yet understood by very few. The word is *Prayer*.

It is probably true to say that every so-called Christian, not to mention members of many other religions, claim to "pray" daily. Yet the sad truth is that very few people really pray at all today in the deepest and best sense of the word. Almost all go through a form of words, silent or spoken, directed to a Being not visible to the eye, yet believed to be "listening in".

There is a form or pattern to this "prayer" which is very recognisable. A mingling of "praise" or perhaps "thanks"; a type of self-condemnation or "confession", and a list of requests or "petitions". Occasionally all this breaks down into a desperate cry for help or guidance. In the case of "Christians" there is added or used in place a "ritual" prayer, alleged to have been taught by Jesus Himself. It is not the object of this article to condemn all this — far from it. Any modern psychologist would tell you (even if he himself were irreligious) that such prayer can have a comforting and uplifting effect upon the people who use it. He would also be the first to admit that "answers" to such prayer are not uncommon. The Church bears witness to the fact of answered prayer right down the ages, and tens of thousands of its members could bring forth startling testimonies of its truth. Yet in spite of all this, the *truth* of the matter is that *very few people really pray. Very few people understand just what true prayer is.*

In the Old Testament we read many such phrases as: "God spoke to Abraham"; "Elijah called upon the Lord" and so on. The latter phrase conjures up a vision of a man with eyes and hands raised up to heaven in "prayer" — the former may have all sorts of effects — a voice speaking out of thin air; an angel or spirit appearing for a moment with a message; or merely an inward "awareness" or intuition. In fact, both are attempts to convey the idea of *prayer*, for prayer is *communication.*

To go down on one's knees; to attempt to penetrate the great unknown, and to pour out one's inmost thoughts or desires in a great emotional outburst is good psychology. It can, in fact, produce startling effects. But it is not necessarily *prayer*, and often is definitely not, for prayer is communication, and the essential meaning of communication is "to share". *Telling* is not communication. *Giving* is not communication. Communication involves an intelligent awareness on the part of at least two "people".

If Christianity were no more than a mere superstition this chapter would be a sheer waste of time, for superstition is unreasoning. We live in an age of reason and of great scientific achievement, yet in the realm of religion, most people adopt an attitude which is quite unrealistic and little more than mere superstition. Let us look at a few examples of this, for they have a great bearing on this subject of prayer.

Christians believe, for instance, that God is omniscient — that He knows all things, even the secret thoughts of every heart. Yet they find it necessary to explain in the minutest detail to Him, their problems, their desires and their hopes. They believe that God is Love, and accept the teaching of Jesus that "whatsoever ye shall ask in my Name, it shall be given to you". Yet they beg and plead with God as if He were unwilling or needed to be persuaded. They believe that God is omnipresent — that He dwells within the heart, yet they "lift up their eyes to heaven" as if He were afar off. They speak of "prayer", which is a two-way communication, yet they usually sign off with an Amen without ever waiting to see if God has anything to say in return.

Surely it is clear that we need to do a lot of new thinking about this matter. It is not that this modern generation has brought forth some new idea which has to be accepted — it merely tells us to use our intelligence and to look again at certain ideas that have been in the world for many hundreds of years — even before the advent of Jesus Christ.

For instance, the prophet Isaiah said: "They that wait upon the Lord shall renew their strength. They shall mount up with wings as eagles; they shall run and not be weary; they shall walk and not faint". Note carefully; he did not say "They that *talk* to the Lord". The whole suggestion behind his words is "They who *listen* to the Lord".

The Psalmist drives home the same thought a dozen times, saying again and again "Wait upon the Lord", and finally, as if impatient with our restless and fevered groping — "*be still* and know that I am God".

Prayer is the secret of spiritual fulfilment. It is the key to spiritual power. It is the very basis of spiritual understanding. Knowing about God is one thing. It is obviously very important, but *sharing with God* (and this is what prayer means) must be infinitely more important and more rewarding.

Now there is nothing to prevent any person from entering into this kind of communication with God at any time. But most of us, through sheer inexperience, come so timidly into a real spiritual experience that we need help. Even Jesus frequently felt the need of support as He entered into His sessions of prayer, and we read that He often took with Him His most valued friends, Peter, James and John. More than once He hinted that where two or three were gathered together (for prayer), they would find help and inspiration.

It has been the experience of the prayer circles mentioned earlier, that when a small group sit together around a table earnestly seeking communion with God, they enter into a spiritual experience which is quite unique. The certainty of the presence of God — or perhaps the presence of Jesus as a more understandable revelation of the nature of God — is a marked feature of their meetings. The necessity for words vanishes, and there is a clear consciousness of *sharing with one who knows.*

What is perhaps even more important, is the fact that, again and again, they are left with unmistakable convictions about what *they must do* about the people or matters that have formed the subject of their prayers. God very definitely works *through* people, and those who dare to pray must be prepared to be *used* by God.

The experience gained in these prayer circles enables every individual to enter into a more realistic experience on the level of their own private and personal prayer life.

In these days few Churches have any big response to invitations by their ministers to hold "prayer meetings". Perhaps this is no great loss until more is understood about prayer. The usual thing in a so-called prayer meeting, is for a few people to "pray" aloud, and other members, present largely from a sense of loyalty, to listen. In most Churches it is usually the same few people who, week by week, lead the prayer, and even the very content of the prayers does not alter greatly. The writer speaks from fifty years of experience of this type of thing, many of them spent as a minister.

Earnest as the minister and people may be on these occasions, they usually fall far short of the true potential of such a meeting. Those who pray aloud are usually people who have an irresistible urge to be heard (not so much by God as by the public), and those who form the rest of the meeting are earnest and devout but without a true understanding of the real nature of prayer.

It is not denied that these meetings have certain good effects. There is always sufficient genuine love and concern for the needs and sufferings of other people to be effective in bringing a certain measure of help to others, and uplift to those taking part. God does not despise our meanest efforts. But oh what greater miracles would be experienced if only we learned to use aright the great power that is available to us.

We have yet to learn a tremendous amount about the full potential of a human being — especially about what might be called his spiritual potential. It is a fact well understood by scientists today that the average man does not use even twenty per cent of his potential, but in few things is he less efficient than in the use of one of the greatest powers God has given him — *The Power of Prayer.*

3

Finding God

It may well be that many people, having read the preceding chapter, and having thought deeply on the matter, may be prepared to accept the ideas that were there outlined, yet find themselves faced with a difficulty — the difficulty of "finding God".

There is, of course, an obvious answer to this dilemma, and one that is backed by experience. It is simply this. God desires to be apprehended, and He will not hide Himself from the earnest seeker. In the fourth chapter of the Book of Deuteronomy, written nearly three thousand years ago, are these very significant words:

"If ye shall seek the Lord thy God, thou shalt surely find Him — if thou search after Him with all thy heart and with all thy soul".

Again, in the first Book of Chronicles, chapter twenty-eight and verse nine, it is written:

"For the Lord searcheth all hearts and understandeth the imagination of the thoughts, if thou seek Him, He will be found of thee".

Nevertheless it is the experience of many people, even of devout Christians, that there are times when they cannot seem to make any contact with God at all. As a minister, I have been told this by hundreds of my people. And quite apart from these cases, which might be termed "temporary blockages", there are thousands who devoutly desire a true spiritual experience, yet cannot seem to find it. I have had this said to me by an earnest young man, and I quote literally:

"If there is a God, He must know that I want to believe in Him, and that I want to serve Him. Why doesn't He give me a sign?" This chapter is written to help those who are confronted with such a difficulty as this.

The first important fact to be noted is this; that the people who claim to be looking for God are nearly always looking in the wrong places. They receive little comfort from such platitudes as; "You can see God in nature — in all lovely things". Of course that is true enough, but they are not looking for evidence of God, *they are looking for God*. But they are apt to be looking for Him in heaven (wherever that is

16

supposed to be). Or in "Space", or even in Church. In fact, anywhere outside themselves, when the truth of the matter is that they must look *inward* if they would find God.

There is a tendency among most people to confuse the terms "Power" and "Size". The idea of a God who is all powerful, who has in fact created the entire universe and is omnipotent, creates a vague idea of great size — even though such a God may be invisible. The Earth is but a small planet revolving in orbit around a very minor star or sun. There are a thousand million stars in our own particular galaxy, and there are a thousand million galaxies. If God created all this, then He must be greater than His creation, and the human mind reels before the implications of such a conception. Some are apt to shrug off the whole effort by saying: "It is a waste of time for the finite to attempt to comprehend the Infinite".

Now one of the most important discoveries of the twentieth century, is that size and power do not necessarily bear any relationship to each other. When, a hundred and fifty years ago, Dr. Gaul said: "Other things being equal, size is the measure of power", there were probably few who would have disagreed with him. Today we know that the greatest power we have yet released is to be found in a thing too small to be seen under any average good microscope.

It used to take hundreds of tons of coal to propel a large liner across the Atlantic from Britain to America. Today we know that atomic "fuel" the size of a single lump of coal, would propel the liner both ways.

One of the early problems in the design of the aeroplane, was that to create an engine powerful enough to lift the plane off the earth involved such added weight as to increase instead of solve the problem — all because a "powerful" engine had to be a "big" engine. Early radio sets increased in size as more and more valves and wires were added to increase "power". Today, with the aid of transistors, an equally powerful radio can be carried in the vest pocket.

So we come to see that "size" is nothing in itself. Size used to be measured by the amount of "space" a thing occupied. But space is rapidly being annihilated in this modern age of speed, and there is every evidence that within the next century, travel at the speed of light will be a possibility.

In the light of all this we can begin to accept the idea that we do not violate the conception of an all-powerful God when we visualise Him as "dwelling" within the heart of a man.

But now let us go a little further. To every individual, nothing can exist which is beyond the reach of his own imagination. To a totally deaf man there can be no such thing as sound, even though he may become capable of producing music (for others) as a purely mathematical exercise. Every new thing which is made by man must be "seen" first of all in the mind of man (the imagination). By means of the power of speech and writing, a man is able to communicate (share) his imagination with another person, and there seems to be a natural urge for men to do this. The matter goes even further. Most people seem to have a natural urge, in fact, an almost irresistible urge to "force" their imaginations upon others — to get them to agree upon the same image. This may well be an innate drive towards harmony, and it breaks down only at the level of *communication*.

Nevertheless it seems obvious that at this stage every person's imagination is intimately his own. It may be closely linked to another's, depending upon the degree of perfection of the communication, but it will not be the *same*. It therefore follows that one man's God can never be quite the same as another man's God. Perhaps it would be more accurate to say that one man's conception of God can never be the same as another's. This will remain so until a term, a quality, an ideal, be found which is common to all — a common denominator. Is there such a thing?

The Christian idea of God as a Father is excellent, but it does not quite fill the bill because every person's idea of a father will be coloured by both experience and heredity. A general agreement would be impossible. A Power; an Intelligence; these are terms which lie wide open to a far greater variety of interpretation. There is only one term which comes near to the *ideal*, and that is *love*.

So when the Apostle John said that God is Love, he came nearest to conveying a thought which might be identical in the minds of vast numbers of people. There is still, however, the difficulty that no matter how real and full of meaning the idea of *love* may be, it is still a "disembodied" reality.

This is where Christianity can fill the need of the world. It gives this very ideal *in the flesh* in Jesus Christ. "He that hath seen me hath seen the Father". Here is something which adds "personality" to the idea of love. Here is something which, allowed to dominate your imagination, can be not only "Your" God, but the God of all men.

This, then, gives us a starting point in our "search" for God. We at least know "what" we are looking for. Jesus was the full and final revelation of the character of God. But Jesus was *in the flesh*. God reduced, as it were, to the size of man so that we might begin to understand — and this, as we have shown, does no disservice to the God of all creation.

It will pay us at this stage to look back into the past so that we may see all this in the right perspective. Running like a golden thread through the whole of the Old Testament is the promise that "One would come" to make clear the nature and purpose of God. But even before this, the writers of the early part of the Book of Genesis — or to be more exact — the story tellers upon whose tales the early historians built the Genesis story, showed exactly what was the nature and purpose of God. There is, perhaps, no writing which, down the ages, has been so tragically misunderstood as the early chapters of Genesis. So let us start right here and see if we can pick up the threads.

After a brief passage in which an attempt is made to describe how God created the Universe — and we shall go more deeply into this matter later in this book — we reach a point where *man* first comes into the picture. I believe that here, although the writer of the second half of the first chapter of Genesis does not go deeply into the matter, he hints at a tremendously important aspect of the character of God. Let me put this into a simple and straightforward form that all can understand.

God has created all things. The sun, the moon and the stars; the dry land and the water; the plants and flowers and living creatures which live in every part of the vast Universe, *but God is alone* with his creation. Have no doubt whatever that God experienced a feeling of utter *loneliness*. Everyone who has ever created anything, from a poem or painting to an architectural design for a cathedral, from a book to a battleship, knows that there is no satisfaction until the achievement can be shared with some understanding person. That "feeling" is part of God's creation and He could not create what He had not experienced. So, because He is alone with His creation, God goes a step further: "Let us create man in our own image". This cannot be read any other way than that God is saying: "Let there be a co-equal, with whom I can *share*". Man was not to be just another puppet to respond when certain strings were pulled. Not something that *had to think exactly like God*, but that *could* think like God. To achieve this aim, man *had* to have the freedom to decide for himself — but the purpose of God is abundantly clear.

The story goes on in chapter two to show how God made provision for man to find an alternative to sharing with God, and an answer to his own consequent loneliness. It shows how God made wonderful promises to man, but promises which were largely conditional. It was almost as if God were saying: "Fill *my* need and I will supply *all yours*", and indeed, this puts the whole situation into a nutshell. Come into perfect harmony with God and all things are possible. The perfect fulfilment and the perfect happiness of man depends upon *sharing with God*. He Himself desires this above all things, but He will not *compel* it.

As the Genesis story unfolds, we see how man chose wrongly and how, as a result, he lost contact with *reality*. He became so out of harmony with God that he no longer understood Him at all. There follows a long story of man's groping for the *truth*, and of his experiments with "religion". Of a *fear* which grew out of the loss of understanding, and the *need* to get back to the starting point.

In a sense, the story starts all over again with the coming of Jesus. In the last two thousand years we have seen history repeating itself, even to the point where many believe that the urgent need of the world is "*The Second Coming of Christ*".

Does all this help you to find God? At least it should make this salient point very clear. "God is not far from any one of you". Indeed He is *within*. Don't be misled by the quotation: "Behold, I stand at the door and knock". This does not mean that God is *outside*. It is the *inner* door at which He knocks. He and all His power is *locked* within you *waiting to be liberated*. What God wants is a perfect *sharing* — "If any man open the door . . . I will sup with him and he with me".

The very yearning which you experience as you "search" for God is the same yearning which is experienced by God as He waits for the *truth* to dawn upon you.

God will not "force the issue" by going contrary to His own *immutable laws*, and "work a miracle" (that really means something contrary to natural Law). The initiative must come from you. The human cry "*give me a sign*" is, to use a crude expression, merely throwing the whole thing back in God's lap. "*They that seek me with all the heart and with all their mind and with all their soul — will surely find me*".

A very wise man once said: "To be seeking God is already to have found Him".

4

Sharing or Discord

In an earlier chapter it was explained that Prayer was really communication — between man and God. An attempt was made to prove that communication with God could not fail to result in a release of *power*. Let us therefore, look further into the whole question of communication.

No other creatures on earth have developed such extensive and intricate aids to communication as homo sapiens. Even our nearest relations, the apes, have never come within miles of such perfection of means. In facial expression, gesture, speech, the use of instruments and the ability to write; the space destroying telephone and radio, music and art, and even the perfection of a means whereby even the blind may read, we have in our hands the most perfect, useful and adaptable tools for communication.

Yet, if we take the word in its truest meaning of *sharing*, we must admit that our ability to discover, develop and perfect the means of communication has far outstripped our willingness to *share* in the best sense of that word.

Selfishness is possible, and indeed present and detectable in almost all forms of active life, and it is not difficult to trace the relationship between selfishness and disagreement among the higher forms of animal life. But surely the world does not hold any other creature who has developed the "art" of disagreement to such an extent as the human animal.

According to Desmond Morris, the biologist and author of *The Naked Ape*, there is world-wide evidence that animals do not fight or "fall out" so much today as they did centuries ago, and when they do, they rarely finish by killing the object of their quarrel. There appears to be a gradual reduction of selfishness and an increase of communication.

In man, on the other hand, there is a vastly improved ability to communicate yet little sign of any reduction in selfishness, and, in consequence, as a species, we seem not only able but willing to disagree with members of the human race whom we have never even seen, and who are separated from us by great distances.

It is worth noting here, that if only we study the origin of the word "communicate", which comes to us from the Latin through the French, we see a secondary, or perhaps deeper meaning — "holding things in common".

This, you might say, is only another way of expressing the idea of sharing, and of course you are right, but it has this particular significance, that it takes the mind back to the story of the very beginnings of the Christian Church. We read in the Acts of the Apostles these very important and impressive words:

"And they held all things in common, nor said any man that anything he had was his own".

Put briefly and dynamically, this tells us that *they had learned to communicate*.

It becomes necessary at this point to digress a little, for it cannot have escaped you that all that has been said so far seems to point to the fact that the "Communists" have found the ideal state of human social life. The very name seems to confirm this. And it must be admitted that the early Church was indeed the first form of communism.

Now it may be true that in its early stages, communism was headed in this direction, but unfortunately for mankind, the whole movement took a new and oblique path which has led to its becoming, not man's salvation, but his most dangerous menace.

The term "socialist" is now much more accurate than "communist" for it is no more than a revolutionary experiment in social reorganisation. There is a vast difference between compulsory "division" and voluntary "sharing".

It was said earlier that the highest form of communication was sharing with God, but one of the marks of twentieth century communism is the denial of the very existence of God. We argued that the nature of God was *love*, and that therefore, a strong and inescapable link existed between the terms *love* and *communion*, yet there is no evidence that the communist way of life has resulted in any increase of love, either among communists themselves, or between them and the rest of the world. Communism began with, and has steadfastly maintained, an attitude of condemnation of what they call "imperialism" (the act of taking over and governing smaller communities) yet all the evidence is that they themselves have no less ambition than to take over the whole world.

The clue to this deviation from the original ideal lies in the important fact that true "sharing" begins with "giving". This was the central theme of the teaching of Jesus, and this is the vital heart of "unselfishness". The whole edifice of communism must eventually crumble because its foundation is "take" (from the rich). In other words, it is prepared to share what it does not yet possess, and that is the heart of selfishness.

To return to the rest of the world situation, where strife and discord are evident on every hand, a close look will reveal that almost all the difficulty stems from the fact that man uses his fantastic means of communication, not as a means of "sharing", but of "telling". This does not stop short even of the Church.

There are thousands of disappointed and disillusioned Christians in the world today who are inclined to feel that the Church has utterly failed in its task. They are not quite right in this assumption. I am reminded of an old saying by a very wise man: "Christianity has not been tried and found wanting — it has just not been tried". There is a great deal of truth in that assertion.

The facts of history do not support the charge of utter failure on the part of the Church. A very great portion of the social progress of the world has had its origin in the teaching and selfless service of the Church of Christ. The abolition of the slave trade; the emancipation of women; the banishment of child-labour; the building of hospitals; the care of the aged and of the insane; the improved conditions of human labour; these and many other advances have been born out of Christianity. But it is true that, to a very large extent, the Church has lost sight of some of the most important teachings of Jesus, and misinterpreted many others.

Down the centuries the Church has undergone a subtle change. The original conception of Jesus, for instance, was that we should ease our "neighbour's" burden by taking it upon our own shoulders. The present attitude of the Church is to "tell" the burden-bearer a better way of disposing of his burden. Jesus had a genius for getting to the very heart of a situation and dealing with *causes*, and not with *effects*. The Church almost invariably puts the cart before the horse by spending endless energy and money upon the treatment of "symptoms" instead of "diseases".

To take a single example; strong drink is a serious world problem today, and none can deny the misery and unhappiness, and even loss of life which are the results of the misuse of alcohol. The Church recognises the evil, and for as many years as one can remember, has directed vast sums of money and a vast amount of energy in campaigns aimed at abolishing liquor. The only visible result is that more strong drink is sold and consumed today than ever before in the history of the world. The problem is not getting less but greater.

Can this mean that the efforts, the sacrifices, the service and the prayers of tens of thousands of Christians are being ignored by God? Rather, the truth of the matter is that all this effort and expenditure is being spent on the treatment of a "symptom", and little is being done about the discovery and treatment of the disease that produces it. It would probably be nearer to the truth to say that thousands of Christians are spending their time daily in "telling" God what to do about the problem, when they should be "listening" to Him so that He can use them in the right way in order to solve it. It is very true that "without God, man cannot — without man, God will not".

Suppose for a moment that the Church had its way — or, to put it crudely, that God gave way under pressure and granted the request that drink be abolished — would that solve the problem? The experiment of American prohibition should be a good enough answer. The real point is that "drink" is a *symptom*. I have no desire here, and at this moment, to discuss the separate and specific problem of alcoholism as a disease.

Let us suppose that in a single specific case a man is unhappy in his home. He has some mental block which makes it difficult for him to understand his wife or to have patience with his children, or to enjoy his work. He takes to the "bottle" and finds artificial comfort by "dulling" his mind. Are we going to solve this man's problem by snatching the bottle from him? Far from "saving" him, we will in all probability "destroy" him. Alcohol may be superseded by drugs, and suicide or worse may take the place of drugs. He does not need someone to *preach* at him. He needs someone to *communicate* — some understanding soul to get alongside of him and to *share* with him.

As you break this whole problem down in this way, and look at it, not with a wide-angle lens, but under the microscope, you will see that the Church, as a vast organisation (ever seeking to improve its efficiency as an organising machine) is bound to fail. But see the Church as a great number of *individual cells* charged with the business of getting alongside of people in need and *sharing* with them, and you will begin to see God's redemptive *love* in operation.

If the Church fails to set the example, it is little to be wondered at if the world at large falls down on the question of communication. It seems that so many people know (or think they know) how to organise other people's lives — though they fail to get the best out of their own.

On every hand we see organisations busy with the business of making this world a better place to live in. Perhaps there never was a time when so many people were filled with good intentions, yet the peace of the world never hung upon so slender a thread. Look more closely at these organisations and you will see that here, too, there is usually a break down in communication. One is tempted to wonder whether, perhaps, man is naturally a selfish animal, and that it is as impossible to change him as for a leopard to change his spots. But if you take a closer look you will see that this is not really so. The Church (and that means millions of people) *genuinely desires* to make this world a better place. The social organisations *really desire* to improve the lot of mankind. The Peace Councils *fervently desire* to put an end to war for ever. The educationalist *desires* to teach.

It is no accident that the human animal learns more rapidly in the first tender weeks, months and years of its life than at any other time. It is because its tutors (mainly mothers) "get alongside" and *share* the knowledge they are trying to impart. Any observer will tell you that in later life, the really successful teacher is the one with such a love for children or people that he is able to *share* his knowledge and not merely *poke it* at his pupils from a distance. It is true that we learn much under the whip of fear, but we learn infinitely more under the sweet influence of *love*.

This very chapter, and indeed this whole book, would come under exactly the same condemnation as a failure to communicate but for two things. Firstly, it is the product, not merely of the writer's personal thinking and conclusions, but of a small group of Christians who thought it worth while to get together to *share* a common concern for others; remained together to *share* the real joys of fellowship and love, and in doing these things found at last a way to *share with God*.

Secondly, and this is not so much a reason as a hope; this book, designed as a means of *sharing* with the readers the experiences of the prayer circle, may prompt *you* to *share* with other people. If it does not do that, it will also have failed. Each Circle of Prayer is only able to share directly with such people as it is able to touch. By using the medium of the printed word to reach further afield, it has no desire to press its opinions or convictions upon other people. It desires merely to share with them its experiences. The final choice will always be with *you*. No person can be "saved" by force — not even by argument; nor can they be made happy by any external pressure.

5

Miracles

There used to be quite a common expression: "The age of miracles has ceased". If there had ever been a vestige of truth in this assertion, one might have been tempted to ask: "When did it begin?" for evidence of "miracles" goes back as far as there are any records of mankind.

Of course the statement is utterly false. It is merely a careless grouping of words without any real thought behind them. The miracle of Creation has not yet been explained away convincingly by any scientist or philosopher, and at the other end of the scale, such things as men visiting the moon, doctors fitting new hearts for old and coloured television pass almost unnoticed in our present age.

It becomes necessary to define what, exactly, we mean by a "miracle". The dictionary, however, is not very helpful here. It says that a miracle is anything that happens which is contrary to natural law. But can anything happen at all if it is contrary to God's *law* — and that is surely what is meant by "natural" law? Obviously not.

What we really seem to mean by a miracle is "anything which is unexpected, or which man cannot explain away by the very limited knowledge which he has at his command". When any such thing happens, man invariably begins to seek the unknown law to which it has been obedient.

Radio and television would certainly have been regarded as miracles by the people of the nineteenth century, though they are quite commonplace to us now that we understand the laws by which they work. Even a few years ago, for anything to "drop" upwards would have been regarded as a miracle, but today it is commonplace to space travellers. Yet in spite of all this, it seems to be the common experience of man to resist and to doubt any new thing.

Take, for instance, the "miracles" of healing recorded in the New Testament history of the ministry of Jesus. More people have been concerned with the business of trying to "explain them away" than have ever been devoted to the task of finding the *laws* under which they operated.

27

Too many people have been prepared to accept them in what they call "faith", and yet to write them off as things of the past — thus giving rise to the very saying with which this chapter opened: "The age of miracles has ceased".

Let us try to look at this matter objectively, and to make some comparisons between "miraculous" healings and other phenomena which we now accept without hesitation.

If you cut your finger with a razor accidentally, certain damage is done to the skin and flesh, and this will need some kind of repair. Knowing the dangers of infection, you will probably sterilise the wound and bind it up. Maybe you will also use some well known ointment to help the healing process. But you will know by sheer experience that several days, or even weeks may be necessary for the process of healing to become completed.

Now all the resources for the repair of skin and tissue lie within the human body. No doctor on earth could heal a similar wound made, for instance, in a piece of beef steak. Within a few days, in ninety per cent of cases, the wound will heal and the finger will be as good as new. The important thing about all this is the time element. If the finger heals within a few days you will not be in the least surprised. If, on the other hand, the wound healed within thirty seconds, you would say that a miracle had taken place. Anyone not actually being an eye-witness of the occurrence would doubt your word, or at best put it down to your vivid imagination.

Now turn your thoughts for a moment in another direction. Until a few years ago the world accepted the fact that sound travels at the rate of approximately a quarter of a mile per second. The sound of a gun, fired a mile away, would not be heard by you until about four seconds later. This was accepted as a law of nature and it still holds true. But by using other laws which run parallel, we also know that *we do not have to wait* four seconds to hear that gun. In fact, we can hear sounds made thousands of miles away *instantly* by means of radio. In other words, the *time factor* is not infallible. Now why should it seem ridiculous to assume that if we knew how to operate the right *laws*, that a wounded finger might also be healed instantly?

Perhaps you think that this is far-fetched, and that there is really no point of comparison between the two examples. Then let us take the matter into the realm of positive and provable experience.

If you took a sharp blade and pierced your cheek with it the blood would rush out, and you would have an unsightly wound which would need all the careful attention that you gave to that cut finger of our last example. Yet a qualified hypnotist could put you into a light trance, pass the sharp bladed knife through one cheek and out at the other without shedding a single spot of blood, and healing so instantly and perfectly that there would be no visible sign at all.

This has been demonstrated in public in the presence of unimpeachable witnesses, and I have seen it done personally. Yet it is not so strange after all because thousands of ordinary observers will testify that devotees of certain religions regularly perform similar feats *without* the help of any hypnotist and yet with precisely the same results. Now it is impossible to do this without causing a wound, therefore the wound must be *healed instantly*.

Thus, ignoring for the moment the *laws* under which this happens, we have no alternative but to believe that *instant healing is possible — and it does take place*. It should be no more an occasion for surprise than the fact that a man *can* visit the moon, or that he *can* sit in his lounge and listen to a concert taking place a thousand miles away.

Having established the fact that under certain circumstances, healing can take place instantly, let us take a closer look at the whole question of sickness.

What, exactly, is sickness (or illness, to use a better word)? It is that state in which the body or mind is not functioning as it should. For some reason or other, the various parts (organs, cells, functions —call them what you will) are not working harmoniously together as they are intended to do. In fact, to put it very briefly, the person — the word being used to include body, mind and spirit — *is not in harmony*.

A doctor may use all sorts of different scientific terms to describe the state. He may speak of "a hardening of the arteries"; of a "virus infection"; of a "slipped disc"; of "cirrhosis of the liver" or a thousand other things, but he would be the first to admit that there is no better inclusive term than to say that the patient is "out of harmony".

The doctor's business is to restore the harmony. If the disharmony is caused by the presence of "foreign" bodies in the blood stream such as an invasion of certain germs, then he will take such steps as are known to help to repel or drive out such invaders. If a bone is broken he will set it in its original condition as far as is possible to aid the body in its own special work of knitting the bone together again. If there is some chemical imbalance, he will administer such corrective chemicals or "medicine" as may be necessary to restore the balance.

Doctors, however, go much further than this. If parts of the body are so out of harmony that they represent a "danger" to life, or so seriously affect other parts as to greatly aggravate the sickness, they very frequently "operate" to cut away these offending parts. Or if the tissue etc. is so affected that there is no *known* cure, they may order the removal of the offending portions of the body.

We may speak of all this as the science of healing, and it is a relatively new science. Its development has been almost as rapid as the development of electronics. When we remember that the history of the human race goes back millions of years, and the history of medicine no more than a few thousand, it would be presumptive to imagine that all the right answers have yet been found, or to reject the possibility that the *direction* of its researches could possibly be wrong.

When heavier-than-air machines were first used for flying, almost all the research was directed towards defeating the force of gravity. In other words, it was directed *against* one of nature's *laws*. One day an aero-engineer lay on his back at the seaside, watching the sea gulls cleaving the sky with supreme grace and lack of effort, and he remembered that sea gulls are also heavier than air. "Suppose", he thought, "that instead of fighting against nature, we learned to co-operate *with* nature . . ." This was the turning point in aero-engineering.

The human body is a most fantastic piece of machinery and not the least of its wonders is the fact that it was "designed" to be self-servicing. Built into it are all the resources and the "know-how" to deal with any attack from "germs" or other perils except certain violent poisons and sudden "breakage" such as is caused by violent accident or high explosive. *But it was designed to operate according to certain laws.* Any attempt to violate those laws will end in disharmony if not actually in disaster.

We cannot doubt that medical science has already seen this point. A few years ago a simple operation for the removal of an offending appendix, involved the patient lying in hospital for about six weeks. Today the patient is encouraged to get up and *walk* on the second or third day after the operation, and is rarely in hospital for more than four or five days. As in the case of aircraft, co-operation *with nature* increases efficiency and also adds *speed* to the process.

To digress a little while still thinking of the *time element*, the resurrection of Jesus has been completely misunderstood by most people. There is a mountain of evidence that on the third day after the crucifixion, the body of Jesus was no longer in the tomb where it had been placed — *in spite of the fact that it could not have been stolen.* There is, however, *no evidence* that Jesus, in that body, ever emerged from the tomb.

According to such laws of nature as we are familiar with, it would have taken years for the body to decompose so completely as to leave no trace behind. *But Jesus, for several years, had been using less familiar laws to bring about cellular and structural changes in human bodies — with the object of healing them.* Dare we not assume that such laws were brought into use by Him to dispose of His now useless body? The Gospel story, in fact, gives us a very pointed clue in this direction. Look at the written evidence of one of the eye-witnesses recorded in John 20: 6-7.

"Peter . . . seeth the linen clothes lie, and the napkin that was about His head, not lying with the linen clothes, but wrapped together in a place by itself".

We are left with no doubt that the body had "dissolved". Had Jesus walked out in that body, the grave clothes would have gone too, or, if discarded, would have dropped in a pile or have been scattered about the tomb.

There is the further evidence that the disciples on the way to Emmaus did not even recognise Jesus. It was not dark as they walked, and the journey could not have taken less than one and a half hours, *and their minds were full of the subject of Jesus. Yet they did not know him.* Of course! The old familiar body was gone. It was finally disposed of in the tomb, and Jesus was now in an *unfamiliar* spiritual form.

Again, you see, it is the time element that confuses us. We are apt to forget that *time,* as we know it, was "invented" by man to enable him to understand and keep pace with the progress of life *measured by the standard* of such natural laws as he had observed — for instance the so-called rising and setting of the sun. The seasons, regulated (though he did not know it at the time) by the regular orbit of the earth round the sun.

In fact, we have dared to assume for thousands of years, that man-made laws are as inflexible as God's *law* — and this in spite of the fact that we know well enough that every man-made law is broken from time to time, yet God's *law* cannot be broken.

Instant healing should not occasion any surprise; it should rather act as a spur to us to seek more urgently the *law* under which it operates. We shall find as we do so, that the real difficulty lies in the fact that few people will be prepared to accept the conditions of that *law.*

6

The Name

Almost every Christian who prays, finishes his or her prayer with the words "in the Name of Jesus Christ", or alternatively, "for Christ's sake".

This dates back, or course, to the very earliest days of Christianity, and it is another of those phrases which we need to examine closely if it is still to have any meaning to us today.

We cannot doubt that the phrase had its origin in the promise of Jesus, that if we should ask anything of God in His Name, it would be given to us. Only John's Gospel quotes this promise, and it is given to us four times between chapters fourteen and sixteen. A fifth similar promise reads: "At that day, ye shall ask in my name and I say unto you that I will pray the Father for you". John 16:26.

On the face of it, the matter is quite simple. It seems to mean that our prayers to God will gain added power by mentioning the Name of Jesus, with, perhaps, the suggestion that all prayers worded in this manner will pass through Jesus who will be acting in the capacity of mediator. In fact, the Prayer Books of certain denominations frequently use the words (relating to Jesus) "our only mediator".

Casting aside all superstition, to the thinking person such an idea is utterly unacceptable. It reduces God to the level of a mere human whose judgement is liable to be influenced by a clever use of words. And though I have no desire at this point to raise the question of the theory of the Holy Trinity, it makes a mockery of such a theory — placing one part of a single God in the position of pleading with another part of Himself.

At its best, it puts God no higher than an employer whose opinion of a candidate for a vacancy is coloured by the quality of the testimonials submitted.

This is another obvious case where we need to take careful note of the fact that the precise meaning of words is apt to change with the passage of time. We need to ask ourselves the question: "What, exactly did Jesus mean when He addressed the above words to His disciples on the occasion of The Last Supper ?" Are there any clues to help us ?

The phrase *"In My Name"* is significant in as much as it had a deeper meaning in the days of Jesus than it has today. As we examine that meaning we will find also a deeper understanding of what Jesus meant by the phrase quoted in the Synoptic Gospels (Matthew, Mark and Luke) — "Whosoever receiveth a little child *In My Name* receiveth me".

In those days there were no such things as "passports", but it was a very common thing for a traveller to travel "in the name" of his chief or king. That was his safeguard — in a sense, his passport. If, for instance, a man travelled in the name of Sheik Abdullah, it meant that any injury done to him, or any insult offered to him, was deemed to have been done or offered to Sheik Abdullah, and the person responsible could be called to account for it.

There was a deeper connotation, of course. It followed that such a "passport" would only be given to a trusted person who shared the beliefs and interests of the giver. In other words, the traveller identified himself with the person (or *power*) in whose name he travelled.

It may be fairly deduced that what Jesus implied was "anyone who stands for the things I stand for". In Mark's Gospel the matter is made still clearer. In the ninth chapter, the disciples complained to Jesus about a man who was "casting out devils" in *the Name of Jesus*, yet who had not publicly acknowledged Jesus nor become one of his disciples. Jesus showed them clearly, that since the man was doing the same work as Himself, he could not be doing evil; he was, in fact, "on the side of Jesus".

All this, therefore, surely indicates that when Jesus said: "Whatever you ask *In My Name*, it shall be given", He was saying in effect: "When your motives are the same as mine, your prayers will be effective". And this puts a completely different complexion on the whole question of our "praying". An example taken from a recent experience of the writer may help you to see where all this leads.

A young father, who might be classed as an average "Christian", had a baby girl of whom he was naturally very fond. The child became alarmingly sick, and the doctor called in to deal with the illness, was quite unsuccessful in arresting it. The father prayed earnestly that the child might be healed and even called in the help of the Prayer Circle in this direction. After this he became so cheerful that his wife and family accused him of being either callous or uncaring about the child's distress. He defended himself by saying: "I prayed in the Name of

Jesus for my child to be healed. Christ doesn't lie, so I have faith that
the little one will get better".

A few days later the child died and a great bitterness filled the heart
of the father. "How can I ever believe again?" he asked me. "Christ
lied to me and He has let me down. I had a great faith but now it is
destroyed for ever".

A superficial examination of the case might lead us to the same
conclusion, but because we *know* that Jesus did not lie, we must look
deeper so as to find the *truth* of the matter. The young father undoubtedly used the phrase "In the Name of Jesus" in his prayer, but did he
in fact, "identify himself" with Jesus? Were his motives really the
same as Christ's? What, indeed was the *real* prayer that the father
offered (if indeed it was true prayer at all?) Suppose Jesus had been
the father of the child, *how would He have prayed*?

All the evidence we have of the character of Jesus leads us to believe
that under those circumstances He would have prayed something like
this: "Dear Father, I love this child. Make her well again. Nevertheless
Thy will, not mine be done".

Jesus would have loved the child well enough to let her go if God
had some higher purpose for her soul — if God, seeing the end from
the beginning, knew that it was best for the child not to recover. Now
turn your thoughts back to that young father. Was his "prayer" as
pure and unselfish? Was it controlled by the same motive as the
prayer of Jesus? I asked this man the vital question: "Is it not true
that your real heart cry was 'O God, don't take this child away from
me, for I couldn't bear it'?"

In fact, stripped of all sentiment and all self-deception, the man was
not really praying for the child at all — *he was praying for himself*. By
what right could he possibly assume that in dying, the child would
pass to something *worse* than this life? Did he consider for a moment
the fact that, in dying, the child might rise to something higher, or
that, in dragging her back to life, he might be condemning her to
years of suffering or tragedy? Let us put sentiment aside and face the
facts — *he was not praying in the Name of Jesus* at all.

In the example quoted, when all this was pointed out, the father
admitted the truth of these charges, and finally found comfort in the
assurance that God's perfect will is always best. But this does not
entirely dispose of the difficulty. There is another angle which needs
clearing up.

From all the foregoing, it would seem that we are always likely to be *"in the dark"* in our prayers — that there will always be a big *"if"* about them. It has even been suggested that the whole business of prayer is a waste of time because *nothing can be done* which is not *the will of God*. The prayer of Jesus in the garden of Gethsemane in fact, was all a waste of time according to this view. God was going to have His own way in any case, so why try to persuade Him to "change His mind?" If every prayer must be "Your will, not mine" the whole business of prayer seems to be pointless — all we are doing is to ask God to "please Himself" — and He is going to do just that, whether we pray or not.

It does, on the face of it, seem to be a mighty problem to the thinking Christian. But it is only a problem to those who do not understand what prayer really is. We are, indeed, taken right back to one of the earliest observations in this book, that very few people really *pray* or understand *how to pray*.

Before dealing directly with this question, which means going over the old ground again, one other point needs to be noted, and that is *the danger of using words in prayer*. The power of speech was given to us as a means of *sharing*, and *conveying information* is a mere part of this process. It is a sad fact, however, that all too often speech is used, both innocently and intentionally, to hide the truth rather than to tell it.

Too often we say things because *we want to believe them*. We use words in order to deceive ourselves as well as to deceive others, and have no doubt of this, even the most sincere and devout souls use words at times in an endeavour to deceive God. Psychologists will tell you that this is part of a process known as *rationalising*, which goes on *unconsciously* within the mind. Don't think for a moment that this is evidence of sinful intention — it isn't as simple as that, An intelligent person would not consciously try to deceive God, knowing how impossible it would be. An honest person would not consciously endeavour to deceive his friends, and a wise man would not consciously attempt to deceive himself — yet all of them do these things unconsciously to preserve the balance of their minds.

Speech may be one of the most useful assets of the human animal, but it is also one of the most dangerous. Long before the science of psychology had been thought of, James, the brother of Jesus, had at least a glimmering of the truth when he wrote the third chapter of his letter — "The Epistle of James".

But words have nothing to do with real prayer.

7

His Will or Mine

Let us now, for a while, consider the question raised towards the end of the last chapter, concerning God's will and its relationship to prayer.

Amongst the great mass of regular pray-ers, a rather crude idea persists — though they would never for a moment admit the thought — of a God who is a sort of glorified storekeeper, endlessly receiving requests, and deciding whether or not the granting of such requests is "good for the person making it".

Added to all this is a vague idea that if one prays "hard enough" or often enough, the storekeeper may be persuaded to change his mind or give way under pressure. There are times when it is almost impossible to escape the impression that an attempt is being made to "twist God's arm", or a sense of wrestling with a reluctant God.

It is most unfortunate that the parable told by Jesus and recorded in Luke's Gospel chapter eleven, verses five to eight, appears to give a certain authority to this type of prayer. I am convinced, however, that Jesus had in mind an entirely different aspect of prayer which will be discussed later.

As has already been pointed out, this "begging" type of prayer is not entirely valueless. It has a certain psychological value, but in fact it has nothing whatever to do with God. Indeed, in the truest sense, it is not real prayer at all.

If we examine this matter dispassionately, it must be obvious that nothing but the utmost chaos could result from a condition in which God is constantly arranging things and deciding things in response to the pleading of millions of creatures who besiege Him at every moment of the day and night. The truth of the matter must obviously be quite different from this.

All the evidence that has ever been discovered points to the fact that the whole universe is governed by *law*, and that the *law* is reliable and predictable. For every effect there is a cause. God does not make "last minute" decisions. It is true that God has given man freedom of action and freedom of choice (within certain limits) but He cannot be "surprised" nor disconcerted by any action we may take. Every circumstance or combination of circumstances has been legislated for, and nothing we or any other creature can do can cause God to have to make some radical change in His plans or arrangements. Thus it can be said that prayer can only operate as a matter of "cause and effect".

While never losing sight of the fact that God is all powerful, and that we are still in ignorance of many of His plans, laws or provisions, let us make a comparison with what a mere man might do in parallel circumstances. A very simple example will suffice to make the point.

A man with abundant financial resources decides to get married, live in a house and raise a family. He will have a house built with every possible convenience and comfort; he will provide means of transport and communication, and be sure that adequate supplies of food and other necessities are easily available. Then he and his wife will take up residence.

Let us imagine that his wife has not been taken completely into his confidence, and has not had time fully to "explore" her new home. One by one, small problems will arise. As darkness descends on the first night she will need light. The situation has been provided for — all she has to do is to press the correct switch. Water becomes a necessity but needs only the turn of a tap. The opening of the correct door will reveal suitable supplies of food. A telephone provides the possibility of instant communication with other people. The touch of a button floods the lounge with music. Hot water is as readily available as cold. A radiator provides heat and an air conditioner guards against excessive heat. All these things and a thousand others are "laid on". All that is necessary is to be able to operate the correct "controls". The husband is not called upon to rush hither and thither on a last minute scramble to meet each successive need of the person he loves. Because he loved her, he anticipated her every need and made the necessary provision. She has only to operate the right switches.

The success of all this will depend upon certain qualities in the man, and upon certain responses on the part of the woman. The man as the provider or "creator" must have endless resources; there must be no limit to his power to provide. Secondly, he must have such a complete understanding of the woman as to be able to anticipate her every need. And thirdly, he must love her sufficiently to hold nothing back which would increase her well being and her happiness.

The woman, on the other hand, must learn to *use* the things provided;

to operate the right switches in the right manner. She needs to have *faith* in her husband, or she may never get the best out of the facilities provided. She needs to get very close to him and to love him or she may never discover more than a small portion of the wonders that have been provided for her happiness.

Magnify this situation a few million times and you will begin to see how closely it parallels God's dealings with and provisions for His children.

The illustration is not perfect of course. It leaves many things unexplained. There will be the person, for instance, who will say: "This does not explain how God can deal with the situation of two farmers on adjacent farms. Because of differences in their crops and the dates of their planting, there comes a time when one will be ruined if it does not rain and the other will suffer a similar fate if it does. They both pray to God for what they need".

Do you seriously believe that God was incapable of foreseeing the possibility of such a situation arising? — or that God was unable to devise an adequate answer? Let us be quite candid; people whose conception of God rises no higher than that are unlikely ever to be able to grasp the joys and powers provided for their use.

But let us get back to our original problem. We have shown clearly what prayer in *not*. Let us see what prayer really *is*. It has been said that every conceivable situation has been provided for — all that is necessary is to operate the correct switches. Clearly then, prayer must be the vital link between *need* and *supply*. It *is* just that.

It is necessary at this point to draw a clear line of distinction between *needs* and *desires*. There are many people who erroneously believe that happiness consists of having all their desires satisfied, but they are quite wrong. A good parent will be careful to supply all the *needs* of his child, but he will be wise enough not to fulfil all the desires. There is a very human and extremely apt expression which is used to describe the result of giving a child everything he *wants* — he is said to be "spoiled".

Because God has given us such a wide measure of freedom, it is possible for us, by one means or another, to satisfy almost any of our desires, and many do so with disastrous results. But God's concern for us is directed to our *needs*, and He has provided for *every* need. God's will (or God's plan, if you prefer it) is for all our needs to be supplied. Man's will is all too often for all his *wants* to be supplied. The true fulfilment of a man is to be in harmony with God; that means having the same aims, or moving in the same direction. So you can see that what we really mean when we pray: "Thy will, not mine be done", is that we desire to come into *harmony* with God.

A little illustration may serve to explain at least one way in which this works out on prayer. A devout Christian woman had taught her small son to say his prayers every night, and had assured him that "God always answers prayer". One night, as the boy neared the end of his little prayer, he added a special little plea of his own: "Please God, help me to find the marbles that I have lost". When he repeated this request the following night the mother began to be a little perturbed. "Suppose", she reasoned, "he does not find the marbles — will this shatter his childish faith?" For three nights the request was repeated, but on the fourth night the boy never mentioned the marbles. The mother asked: "Did God help you to find your marbles then?" "No", answered the child, "He made me not want them any more". It may be truly said that the child had a greater faith or perhaps a deeper understanding than the more sophisticated mother.

Through all this long discussion we have still been thinking of prayer in terms of *words* — of *asking*. This is almost inevitable because for thousands of years man has been in the habit of translating his thoughts into words as the first step towards their conversion into facts or deeds. Is it possible to communicate without words? Of course it is. Ask any couple who have ever been in love. How blessed have been those hours spent together with never a word spoken, yet with a perfect understanding binding two hearts together. How easily has each understood and interpreted the other's thoughts — and all this, not merely between a man and his mate, but between friends, between father and son, between mother and daughter. Words are so often utterly unnecessary. There is always a danger of words being misunderstood, but the mingling of two minds in perfect love leaves no room for misunderstanding.

Let us go back for a moment to the example of the father and his sick daughter. Here, surely, is a need for prayer — but let us analyse the need. On the one hand there is a child whose body is, for some reason, out of harmony. On the other hand there is a father who has become very attached to the child, who is deeply distressed by the child's suffering and horrified at the thought that he might lose her. That is the apparent situation. But there is much more to it than that. What does it represent in terms of *need*? And how can prayer be used to alleviate that need?

First of all there is the need of the child. In this case, there are no
desires to confuse the issue, except a purely biological urge to hang on
to life and to get rid of pain, because the child is too young to *think* for
herself. The child has had little or no experience of life, no expectations,
no attachments except again the biological attachment to the mother.
In fact, since the child has not yet reached the age of "conscious"
control, *nobody* can know its need but God Himself. And since God
sees the end of all things as well as the beginning, He is the *only* judge
of what is *best* for the child.

In the case of the father, there is a much more confused situation.
His desires are two-fold and simple — that the child shall be relieved
of pain or suffering, and that he himself shall not be robbed of a
treasured possession. But what of his *needs*? His first need is the
removal of *fear*. It is fear that is upsetting his emotional balance; fear
that he might lose his loved one; fear that the child is suffering more
than she can bear; fear that, if the worst happens, his own sense of
security will be completely shattered, and an unconscious fear that if the
child dies, the link between them will be irremediably severed.

His second need is for *courage*. Courage to be able to face a difficult
and dangerous situation without panic. And the third is a need to
share his burden.

He 'prays". At least he follows a pattern which he believes to be
prayer. He calls out to an *unseen being*, using the Name of Jesus as his
advocate, and in a form of words, lays bare his heartfelt *desires*. There
is a temporary relief, born of his belief that he has done the right thing
and that his request will be granted. But it is short-lived because, after
all, it is no more than a form of words, and basically it was selfish — a
self-centred performance.

Suppose instead, *he had sought God — as a friend or father* — with
no words; no begging or requests to obscure the situation; nothing but
a genuine love for his child and a simple trust in his God! He would
have found *calm* and *courage*, because sharing with God is a two-way
act — as God shares the father's suffering, the father shares God's
power. He would have lost his fear because he would have known that
only the best could happen. In fact *all his needs* would have been met,
and the ultimate loss of his child, if indeed this had happened, would
have been received *not as a betrayal of his trust*, but as an answer to his
prayer.

No words would have confused the issue nor led him astray. He
would not have become estranged from God but drawn nearer to Him.

Reduced to simplicity, the situation was this: the man, through circumstances beyond his control *was out of harmony*. True prayer, and true
prayer alone *always restores the harmony*.

The most important *fact* about our Christian religion is *not*, as so
many people think, that *Jesus died upon the cross and rose again*. This is
a wonderful thing in itself and has, perhaps, an even deeper significance
than many think. *But the most important thing is this:*

*It is possible for us to share every moment of our lives with God. He
made this possible and he desires it above all things.*

8

The Power of Thought

It may occur to the patient reader that this book has an untidy habit of dodging about from one subject to another. The writer has only one excuse to offer for this offence. In the true sense of the word he never set out to write a book in the ordinary accepted manner. There is no special theme, and above all things this work was never intended as a "thesis". It is the product of the *shared* thoughts (or perhaps inspiration) of a group of people who met together at regular intervals as a "Prayer Circle" and were led sometimes by circumstances and sometimes (we believe) by God, to think upon certain lines. We believe that these rather random thoughts are worth sharing with other people — hence this book.

In the previous chapter a good deal was said about prayer without words. It is another sign of how easily words can convey the wrong meaning, that many people take this to mean "silent prayer". Of course it is silent prayer in the sense that there is no sound. But silent prayer does not necessarily mean prayer without words.

The truth is that most people pray silently while still using *words* mentally. Words, words, and more words rush through their minds and have exactly the same power to mislead, to obstruct or to deceive as if they had been spoken aloud.

All that has so far been said would be of no value if this point were not cleared up. *True prayer needs no words*, either silent or spoken. This is not easy, as those who have practiced it will be the first to admit. Let us start from the beginning in order to find exactly where the difficulty lies.

The person seeking a true and silent communion with God usually begins by closing his eyes. Immediately thoughts begin to crowd into his mind. They may begin as thoughts concerned with the particular subject of his prayer, and could be kept there provided that they were translated into silent words. But if not so translated, they have a bad habit of changing rapidly, and in a very short space of time, all sorts of irrelevant thoughts take their place.

In order to chase these unwanted thoughts away, many beginners make a quick surrender and revert to unspoken words. This is a very real and disconcerting experience, and at first glance, seems to defeat the whole idea of silent communion.

The truth of the matter is that in this twentieth century of rush and bustle, where one experience crowds in upon another, where time seems to be so important, man has lost the "art of contemplation". When he does take time off to be quiet, his body may be still and relaxed, but his mind carries on with what is best described as "day-dreaming".

It will be shown in this chapter that, though pleasant and relaxing, this can be a dangerous practice, and is certainly the arch enemy of silent communion. In prayer, the spirit reaches out to God, but at this point the mind usually takes over and upsets the whole process by flashing one picture after another upon the screen until real communion seems impossible. Every beginner needs help, and it is the object of this article to attempt at least to provide that help.

First of all you need courage and patience to continue, or you will never succeed. "They that seek the Lord . . . with all their heart and soul shall surely find Him". The way is not easy. There are no short cuts. Practice and yet more practice is necessary — with the courage to refuse to allow "day-dreaming" to fill your quiet time. The first difficulty is learning to "empty" your mind. Nature, we are told, abhors a vacuum, and this seems to be true of even so insubstantial a thing as the mind. Thoughts rush in unbidden. They must be ruthlessly driven out. If any one of them is allowed to remain, even for a very short interval of inspection, it will take root. As one wise old man expressed it: "I cannot prevent the birds from flying round my head but I can refuse to allow them to build their nests in my hair".

If you are not too easily discouraged, you will find that this process of emptying the mind gets a little easier every time you practice it. Perhaps the best way to prevent unbidden thoughts from entering the mind, is to *fill* the mind with a picture of your own choosing. Imagine yourself sitting with Jesus, watching His face as He talks to you. Get back to this picture every time a new thought tries to drive it away, until at last the thoughts stop coming. Don't fall into the trap of trying to *talk* to Him. Watch Him and *expect* Him to talk to you. This method has been referred to as "the expulsive power of a great love".

The waiting will not be in vain. The time will soon come when He will indeed talk to you. Out of the quietness and the emptiness will come an idea which you will recognise as "not just another thought".

Sometimes it comes so clearly that you might think you have "heard" it. Sometimes it is not even silent *but real words are heard spoken.* When this happens you will be rewarded for all your patient waiting. The disciples had to wait a long while — forty days, we are given to understand — until at last they received the "Power from on High".

From what has been said, it would seem that "thought" is the great enemy. This is not really so of course. It is the control of thought that is the difficulty. Thought is one of the most powerful forces in the universe — but it can be a power for good or evil.

A great number of the actions and functions of the body are controlled by the "unconscious" mind. For instance, you don't have to talk about breathing; you don't have to tell your heart to beat; your kidneys to function or your eyelids to flicker — these things seem almost to be automatic. Your conscious actions, on the other hand, are controlled by thought. Just what is *thought* ?

You will not find the dictionary very helpful here. Something like fifty definitions are given, and none really states the case very clearly. Perhaps the best is "imagination". To think is to imagine — to image-in. This is at least descriptive because almost all thought begins as a sort of "picture" in the mind.

We all say at times, "I think", as if thought were a product of our own mind — an act for which we alone were responsible. But is that really so ? Is it not much more often the case that the thought "comes" to us, and our mind does no more than translate it ? It is no accident that our language contains such expressions as "I was seized by a thought", or "the thought *entered* my mind".

It is true that we also say "I conceived an idea" or "an idea was born in my mind" — but an *idea* is not necessarily identical with a *thought*.

The difficulty lies in the inadequacy of our language. We tend to use the same words to describe entirely different things or processes. For instance, we speak of "giving thought" to a matter, when what we really mean is that we weigh up one thought against another and decide upon their relative values. We use the same word as a noun — something with its own separate identity, as a collective abstract noun, and also as the past tense of the verb "to think", which is an action or process. We also use it to convey the idea of reasoning, which is, in fact, something quite different, and to express an opinion, which is the result of the process of reasoning. Thus it is extremely difficult intelligently to discuss the question of thought without the possibility of becoming hopelessly confused. It is best, therefore, to confine our discussion to that aspect of thought which is best described by the definition "imagination".

The first thing to note is that it is the beginning of the *creative* process. Everything that was ever made by man began as a *thought*. A thought may therefore be likened to a seed, which in some mysterious way, contains within itself the possibility of becoming a vigorous plant. The likeness goes even further. In the words of the Book of Genesis, "it contains within itself also a fruit yielding seed — after its own kind".

Two important facts must be noted here. Firstly, not all seed is productive. Some is never planted, some is planted in such poor soil that it comes to nothing, and some is lost or destroyed. The second fact is, that the seed when planted, brings forth fruit of its own kind. Figs may not be gathered off thistles. A good thought cannot yield evil fruit, and an evil thought cannot yield good fruit.

From all this we see that, although the original seed must have been the product of a "thought", it also has the power to "create" a thought. You will see, of course, where all this is leading. There are obviously at least two categories of thought. There are the thoughts that come from outside the mind (very often unbidden) and there are the thoughts created or produced by the mind. You are, in fact, able to receive thoughts which were not of your own creation, and you are also able to produce thoughts of your own.

When a person speaks, thought is translated into sound, which, as you know, is a vibration of the particles of the medium in which it was originated, (in most cases, the air). If this vibration is "picked up" by the ear drum of another person, we say that it is "heard". We all know that it can be picked up in other ways, particularly by electro-magnetic apparatus, and transmitted over long distances at incredible speeds. But suppose the thought is *not* translated into sound — what happens to it? Is it any less powerful? Is it any less effective?

Too easily most people write it off as if it had no existence or no importance, just because they see no immediate results. But it does have results, and it is important. We know that thought "waves" (if we may call them by that name), can be transmitted just as sound waves are, though we have not yet perfected any device by which this can be done consistently or systematically. Nevertheless we cannot deny the existence of what is commonly called "telepathy", and most people, in a mild way, have experimented with it, and often with considerable effect.

It is clear that the atmosphere is full of thought waves (we use the term for want of a better), just as it is full of sound waves. In a room full of people all talking at once, it is impossible to shut out all sound except one particular person's voice to which we desire to listen. We can be successful up to a point, however, by using what we call "the power of concentration". In this way we "shut off" all other sounds but those we wish to hear.

It is much easier, as we all know, to do this sort of thing with a radio set. Here we are able to "tune in" to the particular programme that we wish to hear. Or we could put it the other way round and say that we "tune out" all the sounds we wish to omit.

This is exactly what we aim to do when we seek communion with God. We cut out all extraneous thoughts, and "tune in" to God.

Why is it that a good man often finds evil thoughts flooding unbidden into his mind? Certainly they are not of his own making, or even of his own choosing. And in the same way, it is certain that, at times, good thoughts enter into the minds of the most evil of people. It is obvious that all kind of thoughts, good and bad, sensible and stupid, helpful and injurious, are "floating" about, and have the ability to enter any mind which is not defended against them, and to take root and flourish if not checked. You will see how important it is for us to be *master* of our thoughts, and not merely victims.

If you would be a *positive* person, you must rigorously exclude every negative thought from your mind. More than one person, and notably Norman Vincent Peale, has written exhaustibly on this aspect of the matter we are discussing. The writer will, therefore, content himself with merely a few important observations.

If the mind is not defended against negative thoughts, they will flourish like weeds in a garden until there is no room for useful and positive thought to develop. For this reason, we should never allow these negative thoughts to be translated into words, for that is the first step towards increasing their power. Do not mentally *argue* with a negative thought, because in so doing you are acknowledging its existence and doubling its power. Expel it as soon as it obtrudes itself. Do not toy with an evil thought, for the next step will be to give it power over your life. This was what Jesus was driving at when He said: "If thine eye offend thee — pluck it out".

A very important thing remains to be said while on this subject of thought. What of the good thoughts? What about the positive thoughts, the creative thoughts — how can their power be best developed?

It has already been said that thoughts are like seeds, and like seeds, not all thoughts flourish and bear fruit. The first necessity is for them to be planted "in fertile soil". Bad thoughts and negative thoughts only harm us when we allow them to take root, but in exactly the same way, good thoughts, or "creative" thoughts are completely wasted unless they are *allowed* to take root. When one good thought after another chases itself through our mind, and is allowed to do nothing but drift (and this is precisely what is happening when we are "day-dreaming") it is harmful in the sense that it fills the mind to the exclusion of all else, while never of itself producing any worthwhile result.

It has also been said that thought gains power as it is vocalised. That is the first step. This seems to have been known by the wise men of thousands of years ago. The Book of Genesis is perhaps despised by certain sophisticated people of our present age because it appears to have over-simplified the story of the Creation. But if you read it sympathetically and with understanding, you will realise what a truly inspired document it is. Less than half a century ago, it was believed by scientists that the Earth and each of the other planets in our solar system, began life as lumps of molten matter thrown off by the sun in its rapid rotation in space, and that they gradually cooled down until they took their present form. Today we know that this assumption (or theory) was incorrect. Observe that according to that early theory, there would always have been *light*, too much of it in fact. But the Book of Genesis says that there was "chaos" and that *darkness* brooded over all. Today we know that this was so, for each solar system began as a great cloud of unrelated particles of matter whirling through space. *And the vast reaches of space are dark.*

The *thought* in the "mind of God" was of *order* replacing chaos, and the first process was the gathering together of the "particles" into various sized spherical bodies by what we think of today as magnetic attraction. By *laws* that we are now beginning to understand, the bigger the body, the greater the heat. The biggest of all in each system attained such a size that thermo-nuclear reaction caused spontaneous combustion, and, *the sun was born.* "God *said,* let there be light".

How clearly does this wonderful Book not only give us a clue to the actual beginnings of evolution, but takes us back much further than any mere scientist could, to the point where it all began — *as a thought in the mind of God,* and shows us the steps in the development of a thought. First the thought, then the *word,* and finally *creation.*

But if thought, even when vocalised, goes no further than the mind, it will expire. It must be *planted* — where? In order to try to answer this question, we need to digress a little so as to examine the human entity, and to see how it is made up.

We know that man is something more than an animated machine. That is what he would be if there were no more to him than a body and a mind. The mind is the "switch-board" or control room that activates the machinery (the body). *There is something else*. A man not only knows but he *feels*. Even the fantastically clever organ which we call the brain, guided by the most efficient of all computors, which we call the "intelligence" does not have the last say. The intelligence may very accurately sum up a situation and recommend a certain course of action, but it is often over-ruled by the *feelings* — we call them *emotions*.

To ensure that a thought (the seed) will grow into a strong plant, it must be sown in the emotions. This is what translates mere intellect into positive action. There is a much used saying which well describes the process: "I set my heart upon it".

From time immemorial man has regarded the brain as the centre of the intellect, and the heart as the centre of the emotions. Although this is not biologically true, it is nevertheless a fact that the heart is the first organ in the body to respond to any kind of emotional stimulus. More will be said about this later.

There is much more to be said about the power of thought, and we shall now consider it under separate headings.

9

Thought and Health

This chapter is concerned with the ordinary functions of the body and will not discuss such matters as "accident" or congenitally imperfect bodies, such as those born with deformities or cerebral malfunction, blindness etc. Such cases as these will be dealt with elsewhere in this book.

The body is a fantastic, self-servicing machine, of a most flexible and adaptable type. It is operated by a "built-in" intelligence which uses an incredibly efficient computor and a switch-board of controls (the nervous system) which, if of the scale with which we are familiar in such man-made installations as the power plant of a large engineering works, would be the size of many city blocks.

It operates efficiently only at a certain temperature, but the thermostat controlling this critical heat is capable of dealing with anything from the sub-zero conditions at the polar caps, to the ultra tropical extremes of a man working at an open furnace door in a boiler house.

An amazingly wide variety of fuel is fed into this human machine, and this is dealt with by a built-in chemistry and synthesis department and channelled to a power plant which, though small enough to be held in the hand, is capable of pumping many gallons of liquid through miles of complicated channels continuously for twenty-four hours of every day *without a pause* for anything up to a hundred years.

Everything about this incredible machine proves that the "Designer" intended it to be *independent* of outside help. It synthesises its own "oils" to lubricate its hundreds of moving parts. It seals its own "leaks": critically analyses every particle of fuel, rejecting and disposing of what is unsuitable. It disposes of its waste products, repairs and even replaces any damaged parts, and what is even more incredible, it systematically renews and replaces *every single cell* (countless millions) as many as ten times during the life time of a single person.

When we examine all this data, the perfection of the design and the almost unbelievable efficiency of its planning, it is surely presumptuous to imagine for one moment that the "Designer" could have forgotten anything, or failed to make allowance for any circumstance or set of circumstances which might be injurious to the "machine".

We have given the name of God to that Designer, and today we know that man is only one of countless millions of wonders which were designed and created, and are maintained by Him. He is intimately acquainted not only with the creatures He has designed, but with anything and everything which can affect them from within or without. There seems to be only one "enemy" not legislated for. That is the effect of deadly poison, accident or explosion. But just because we have not yet observed or discovered a way in which God deals with these things, dare we jump to the conclusion that He has made no provision for them? It would surely be absurd to do so.

You may safely say then, that man's body is a self-servicing machine. It has a built-in capacity to take care of any unusual wear and tear or injury to itself. It also has the built-in knowledge to enable it to use all the facilities that are at its disposal. It seems, on the face of it, that doctors are unnecessary, but we should not be tempted to jump to such conclusions. This book is not another form of "Christian Science".

It is true to say, however, that God equipped us to survive — without outside help — under almost any conditions, and, in fact, for thousands of years we *have* survived even though medical science is but a few hundred years old.

If you have ever studied the theory of the evolution of a species, you will know that, as any species progresses, it often happens that one or another part or function becomes unused and eventually unnecessary for survival. Such a part or function gradually disappears over a period of thousands of years and finally ceases to be a feature of the species (as, for instance, the missing "tail" in humans.)

It is a fair assumption that if humans continue to develop their unique quality of social co-operation to the point where they depend entirely upon "social" help to the exclusion of the gifts of self-help provided by God, there will come a time when they are no longer able to help themselves. Penguins and ostriches are equipped with wings, but for so long have not needed or bothered to use them that they can no longer do so.

Doctors have a very necessary and important place in our social structure, and most of them are sincere and dedicated men whose lives are devoted to the service of mankind. We have come to lean upon them so heavily that it would be dangerous at this point to ignore the service they can render to us. *But there is a better way.* If we take care to *keep in harmony* we are unlikely to suffer any serious illness, and if we are wise, we shall give our bodies the chance to use the equipment which God has provided for our use to fight off or cure any illness which might threaten or attack us.

It is particularly in the realm of health that we can see the power of thought demonstrated. Let us take, for example, the common cold. Any doctor will tell you that it is caused by a "germ", and that it spreads only by infection. Yet, so convinced are many people that sudden changes of temperature will cause a cold, that they have only to sit in a draught or a cold room, or go outside on a cold day without a warm coat, and they will immediately "catch cold".

It is a well established fact that any person who has a special fear of a particular kind of illness, will sooner or later develop symptoms of that very sickness. And the reason is that *fear* is *thought* that has been planted in the *emotions*.

It cannot have escaped your notice that people seem invariably to "catch" the sickness against which they take the liveliest precautions. The reason is simple. The *thought* of that sickness is constantly in their minds. They give it so much recognition and attention that before long it is no longer a thought but an established fact.

It is necessary, at this point, to sound a note of warning. Some people recognise the truth of what has just been said, but try to combat sickness by "denial". If, for instance, they are forced to sit in a draught, they will say to themselves: "I cannot catch cold by sitting in a draught". Too often, they go even further by assuring their friends of the same thing, and are very surprised when a few days later they develop a cold. The truth is, of course, that the thought of a cold has never been absent from their minds. They have merely tried to deceive themselves by a clever use of words.

If the thought of any kind of sickness comes into your mind, you must *banish it* immediately. Don't wait to discuss it, to argue with it, or to rationalise it. Get rid of it immediately. This paragraph naturally only refers to the thought of sickness as applying to yourself. It is often necessary, in fact almost inevitable, that we should think of sickness as applied to other people.

Those who talk most of illness are usually the people who experience a great deal of it themselves, but they are quite wrong when they imagine that they think of it *because* they have had so much of it. The truth of the matter is that they have talked so often and thought so often of sickness that they are *bound* to experience it. The thought of illness is already doubled in power as soon as it is translated into words.

Flee from the company of those who bring up the subject of disease and sickness in every conversation, and never be guilty of doing this yourself. If, by some misfortune, you have had a serious illness or an "operation", do your best to forget everything connected with it. Forget the wards, the sisters, the doctors and the other patients, and do not dwell, either with affection or with horror upon any part of the experience. *Most important of all — do not talk about them.* Discourage every conversation which turns in the morbid direction of sickness, and if these thoughts plague you in your moments of privacy or quietness, be ruthless in your rejection of them. They will come to you disguised in a thousand ways, but if you are resolute, you can win the battle in the end.

Many years ago, the cult of Cooeism was very popular. It was an attempt to control thoughts with words. With some people it seemed to work almost miraculously — with others it failed completely. Let us examine the reasons for this.

Basically it was an attempt to cultivate what is now more commonly spoken of as "positive thinking". If a person had some illness, he or she was told to repeat, as often as a hundred times a day, some such phrase as "Every day in every way I am getting better and better". In a great number of cases this worked admirably, but of course, there were always the odd few who added a silent rider "Am I?" These never had a chance. The intention was to conjure up a picture (a thought) of glowing health and of improving conditions. The whole exercise was concerned with preventing negative thoughts from invading the minds of the patients. It succeeded where the patient was led to examine the condition *hoped for.* If failed when the silent question led him to examine himself *as he was.*

There is another point of failure in this system, and that is when thoughts control the words instead of words controlling the thoughts. For instance, it is *fatal* to repeat such a phrase as "I will not (or cannot) be ill". But it is equally necessary to be careful not to declare an obvious untruth. If you have a headache, no point will be served by declaring that your head is free from pain. Your whole system will rebel against anything so unreliable as to ignore an established *fact.*

Take a good *thought,* clothe it with *words* which give it *reality,* plant it in your emotions — that is, *"set your heart upon it"* and *expect* it to happen, and you will never be disappointed. But remember the words of James the brother of Jesus — "if ye waver — let not that man expect to receive anything".

10

Thought and Happiness

It is said of some careless, happy-go-lucky people that "they haven't a thought in their heads". Of course that is not strictly true, for thought of one kind or another occupies our minds almost all of every day, and a good part of every night. It would be more true to say that, with certain people, no thought *occupies* their minds — it is just allowed to drift through.

To some people who are victims of anxiety, it might appear that such a state is ideal, and perhaps they would give much to be able to achieve it. But let it be said immediately that "day-dreamers" never amount to much in this life. They rarely do anything worth doing, and often do not make any real friends. They may never be serious enough to suffer any actual misery, but neither do they ever experience any real joy. Theirs is a life of half-tones, and true happiness does not come their way.

The "state of mind" of a person very often determines the sort of thoughts which come to him. But it is even more certain that the sort of thoughts that are allowed to *dwell* in the mind, determine what we call "the state of mind". Let us examine the situation carefully to see how thoughts affect happiness — which most people would regard as the ideal state of mind.

In an earlier chapter, it was said that every unwholesome thought should be driven out of the mind before it has time to do any damage. You could be excused for asking the question: "How can I determine the real nature of a thought until I have at least examined it?"

It is a fair question and deserves a thoughtful answer. It must be admitted, for instance, that some thoughts come to us in "disguise" — for all the world as if they were maliciously eager to "trap" us. So true is this that it may help us in our examination to think of thoughts as if they were intelligent entities. And if, at first sight, this seems fanciful and far-fetched, remember that for thousands of years this is exactly what people did. They thought of them as evil spirits or devils — and the master mind that gave them birth as *Satan*.

53

Looked at in this light, the operation of an unworthy thought is very subtle, and the writer of the First Psalm seemed to have this in mind when he wrote of "the man who *walketh* not in the council of the ungodly, nor *standeth* in the way of sinners, nor *sitteth* in the seat of the scornful".

Even after making allowances for the subtle "progression" which is a marked feature of Hebrew poetry, the writer makes his meaning abundantly clear. We conjure up in our minds the vision of a man, strolling past a group of "bad" people. It was, perhaps, unwise of him to pass that way at all, but he may have had no option. Therefore he should have been careful to make no contact with them. However, instead of ignoring them he *stands* and listens to their conversation. Having gone so far, the next step is almost inevitable. We see him *sitting* in their midst. He has become *one of them*.

Now let us get back to the original question. "How can I tell?" *You cannot*. The man in the Psalm couldn't tell what those people were talking about until he paused to listen. It was curiosity that trapped him, and there is a great deal of truth in the old adage that "curiosity killed the cat". That man would have been better off among friends of his own choosing, and in the same way, you will be better off, and much safer, amongst thoughts of your own choice. *Keep the mind occupied* — you can't wear it out. Learn to be always creative, and reject any stray thoughts that seek to distract you. They *may* be quite harmless, but at best, they are seeking to destroy your concentration, and are therefore undesirable.

Paul the Apostle covers the point when he says "Overcome evil with good". Let your mind be so occupied with *good* thoughts, ideals and plans, that the undesirable thoughts cannot get in with the proverbial "thin end of the wedge".

Having taken every precaution against harbouring undesirable thoughts, we come now to the next step, and that is to deal systematically with our thoughts. Even acceptable or harmless thoughts can be a severe liability if they are not dealt with.

Some people accumulate a great number of desirable possessions in their homes, yet, having acquired them, never use them nor display them to the best advantage. The net result is that their homes become untidy and unwholesome. Many people in the same way, allow their minds to become cluttered up, and therefore untidy and unprofitable.

The first principle for acquiring or developing a tidy mind is this: when you have allowed a thought to enter, *do something with it*. The most important aspect of this is that, when God speaks to us, He does so by sending thoughts into our minds. We do not always recognise His voice, but we can be sure of this, that if we persist in ignoring it, He will cease speaking. Therefore, if for no other reason, we *must* do something with our thoughts.

We have three choices of action. We can *plant* the thought, we can *file it for reference*, or we can discard it. There is, of course, another category of thought which cannot be dealt with under these headings. We might call this *subsidiary* thought, or thought which has a bearing upon ideas which we have already adopted or planted. These also call for immediate attention, but that usually means "prompt action". Act upon these thoughts at once and *do not put them off* lest they be lost altogether.

You will know only too well that a very large number of the thoughts that come to us are *trivial*. They are neither good nor bad. But even these can be divided into two categories — the negative and the positive. Those that are negative should be cast out without hesitation. Don't deal with them at all lest they swell up and become important. The rest do not matter unless they come at prayer time, or when you desire to think of something else — then they should be ruthlessly thrown out, as if they were evil.

All this probably sounds terribly complicated, and the person trying to put it into practice for the first time may easily become so discouraged as to think the whole thing impracticable — and give it up altogether. But it is not quite so difficult as it sounds. The secret lies in *choosing your own thoughts*, and choosing wisely.

Begin with *good reading*. This prepares your mind to receive only the best kind of thoughts. Add to this, as often as possible, periods of *contemplation* — on subjects of your own choosing, beginning perhaps, with the subject of the book that you are reading. It is a good thing, when unwelcome thoughts persist — especially when they are of such a nature as to irritate or even anger you, to bring into your mind the thought of lovely scenery; the sea lapping lazily on the shore; a sun-dappled glade in the forest; the rolling veldt and distant hills, and so on. This not only ensures the exclusion of useless thoughts, but has the quality of calming the nerves and giving you a sense of well-being. It was no accident that caused the Psalmist to say; "I will lift up mine eyes unto the hills, *from whence cometh my help*". (This didn't mean that he thought that God was away up in the hills).

The second thing is to keep your reading and thinking *healthy*.

Unless you are training to be a nurse or a doctor, avoid reading about sickness and disease, and avoid morbid books. When you visit the sick, try to see them in their *healed* condition, and avoid talking about their symptoms. Try to turn *their* thoughts to healthier and happier topics. Especially when you pray for a sick person, see that person in your mind as a healed and healthy person.

Thirdly, think on happy subjects. Visualise your ideals and your efforts brought to successful conclusions — being careful that in this exercise you do not fall into the trap of "day-dreaming". Without being merely frivolous, see the humorous side of every situation. Smile often, and wherever possible, mix with cheerful people. It is most important to cultivate *some hobby* (the earlier in life the better).

Follow this advice and you will be surprised what a difference it will make to your life. Your life work, whatever it may be, will become *more* interesting and certainly never a drudge. And you will find an increasing measure of success rewarding your efforts in any undertaking which may be occupying your time. Perhaps best of all, you will finally *master the art of contemplation* — and this means, put plainly, that you will be giving God more and more opportunity to *speak* to you. You cannot *share* with the *Creator* without feeling something of His *power* flowing into your life.

11

Thought and Religion

There is, of course, no sphere of life in which *thought* plays a bigger part than in Religion. The religion of many people, indeed, has no reality at all except as a jumble of not too clearly defined thought. The reason why so many people have no real religion, and why so many others get nothing out of religion, is because they have never troubled to treat their thoughts on the subject very seriously — certainly not in the manner recommended in earlier chapters of this book.

As was said at the very beginning, this book makes no claim to being a *text book* — either on religion or any other subject. But it does have this aim — *to set you thinking*, and there is, perhaps, no subject on earth which *needs* so much clear thinking as this matter of religion.

If religion, in fact, is to do you or anybody else any good at all, it must be put into practice. It should not be merely contemplative; it should be creative. Let us put this quite clearly — true religion is not a thought, an ideal — however lofty, it is an *act*, or a series of acts. Like every other thing, as we have seen, it only becomes real when it is planted in the emotions.

There are, however, many thousands of people whose religion has never gone further than to become vocalised. Religion begins with a thought: a thought so vivid that we call it an "awareness" of a *being* or a *power* outside ourselves, and indeed, outside the Universe, and which created and maintains it. For want of a better name we have called that Being "God" which literally means "The Unknown".

It is unfortunate that for most people, this thought is only "second hand". It comes to them through their parents, teachers or books, and thus, rarely has the impact of a "discovery". Depending entirely upon the locality in which you were born, the thought of God may first reach you with a particular shape or colouring. It may be Hindu, Buddhist, Mohammedan, or Christian, and be part of a theology which is but the fruit of a thought whose origin is lost in the distant past. It is both wrong and dangerous to condemn any one of these "religions".

In the light of all that has been written on the subject of thought, it must be obvious to you that in trying to find the true "religion" one can easily be plunged into the greatest difficulty, and lost in such a bewildering complexity of ideas, as never to be fully satisfied. Is there any way to avoid this confusion? Of course there must be.

Jesus many times hinted that the older and the "wiser" (in a purely earthly sense) we get, the more difficult this search will become. Discussing this very point with His disciples one day, He sorrowfully admitted that "narrow is the way, and few there be that find it". But He did give us a very important clue: "And Jesus took a little child and set him in the midst and said: 'Except ye receive the Kingdom of Heaven as this little child, ye shall not enter therein' ".

There are several interpretations which can be put upon this acted parable, and it is worth while to study them all. But you will find that each one leads to the same answer in the end. Here is another helpful interpretation.

There were crowds of children gathered around, and we can well understand that, to Him, they were all attractive, for He loved the little children. He stepped aside and gathered one of them in His arms. Was it a haphazard selection? Was it a specially attractive child? We have no clue to His method of selection, but it was for some reason (or no reason at all?) *His* choice. Then He set him in the midst.

What does this conjure up in your mind? Do you imagine that Jesus just took up a little child and set him down in the middle of a crowd of strangers, thus frightening the life out of the child? Such an idea is unthinkable. It could not have been like that at all. Jesus took the child in His arms and set *himself* in the midst, and kneeling there, He hugged and comforted the child. Then, looking up at the crowd, He said: "This is the only way".

Let us go back now to the person who is truly seeking God. (a) He is surrounded by a crowd — all sorts of ideas and thoughts, young and old, clever, convincing, attractive, frightening, large and small. (b) First step aside. The crowd will jostle you, and if you are not careful, will choose you rather than allow you to choose one of them. (c) You must choose, but you know not how to choose. Let Jesus choose — even if you do not understand. (d) Now you take that choice and set it in the midst (of your emotions). (e) You love it; that is, you "set your heart upon it".

Is this too difficult to understand? Step aside from all the crowd, with its suggestions, its ideas, and its influence — aside into the silence.

Drive out of your mind every thought but the thought of Jesus — He is there with you as you wait. Then, as you reach out into the silence God will come to you. Not Tom Jones's God. Not the God of the Catholic Church, or the Baptist Church, or the Methodist Church, but *your God*. He is not so big that you cannot find Him — He is there in your arms. Clutch Him close and *love* Him.

The whole Law of life is here. Even science will show you this. In your lifetime the most advanced and sophisticated sciences have discovered that the power of the atom is not *outside* — it is the tiny, invisible nucleus which is the *centre*. The power of the solar system is not outside — it is *the sun*; the centre about which the worlds (or planets) revolve. The power of the universe is not outside — it is the invisible centre about which the galaxies revolve. Yes, trace it all back — it is deep in the centre — *in your own heart*.

We said that religion begins with the awareness of God, and now we would go on to point out that the next step is inevitable — an awareness of dependence. Once we have admitted to ourselves the existence of a Being who created all things, we cannot escape the conclusion that we owe all things to Him. Out of this realisation two other thoughts are born, and these are much nearer to each other than you may have thought: *fear and worship*.

Different people react in different ways to the same stimulus. Some instinctively recognise the wonder and the beauty of life and creation, and feel a deep sense of thankfulness that they are even a small part of it. The awe which fills them is the beginning of Worship.

Other people see nothing but a threat to their own existence in the fact of God; a fear that supplies might be cut off, or that they themselves might be destroyed. This also is the beginning of worship, but of a very different kind. Their worship is merely an act of appeasement — of "getting on the right side of God".

Of course there is a psychological reason for these differences, but we have no need to discuss this at the moment. However, do not let this fact suggest to you that it is something *new*. We can turn once more to the Book of Genesis, which deals, in its own very simple way, with so many psychological problems. For instance, the very question we have just been discussing was apparently recognised a few thousand years ago as one of man's deep problems, and was dealt with in the well known but not often understood story of Cain and Abel.

The story is brief and does not go into detail. It tells us merely that "Abel offered up a more acceptable sacrifice than Cain". At this point we are only concerned with the fact that an awareness of God (the beginning of religion) led to action on the part of the two brothers.

A casual reading of the Genesis story might lead you to think that both Cain and Abel offered sacrifices to God, and that perhaps Cain was a little "niggardly" with his contribution. But this is to miss the whole point of the story. There is nothing to suggest that this was so, except the supposed displeasure of God. The real purpose of the story is to show that, while both sons went through a *form of religious rite*, one was sincere (or real) and the other was not. The religion of Abel led to a certain quality of life, and that of Cain only to the observance of ritual. There is also a very subtle clue given in the explanation that Abel became a shepherd, but Cain an agriculturalist. Abel dealt with living, feeling creatures, Cain was probably a materialist.

We will not, at this point, deal with the question of Cain's resentment which finally led to murder, for this has no bearing on our present subject, but it is worthy of note that Cain (and his like) are for all time doomed never to get the best out of life.

We should have learned this lesson then: there is no such thing as a *passive* religion. The *thought* of God must be creative. It must pass beyond words (and this includes ritual) into *action*. We come back once more to a point stressed in earlier chapters, that thought must be planted in the emotions. In this case, the emotion must be *love* and not *fear*.

Once this is done we are on the right road, for love is never passive. Love, in its fullest sense, can never be regarded as a "state of mind" like contentment or pleasure. It is always active, always *giving*, always seeking.

This leads us to an examination of another state of mind which might be called "self-satisfaction". In Christianity, this usually is recognised as a state of "Righteousness" or perhaps "Holiness". Now this is completely introspective. At best it is self-centred and therefore certainly at odds with the teaching of Jesus which instructs us to "forget self".

If the thought of God is planted in the emotion of *fear*, it will almost inevitably lead to this state. There will be the constant *fear* of doing the wrong thing, a constant *running away* from "evil", a constant "hiding" from the unpleasant facts of life. In fact it is a completely negative attitude to life and represents all the difference between "being good" and "doing good".

It will be shown later how this negative religion militates against the possibility of a true harmony with God, and therefore is heir to all kinds of sickness. But it is sufficient for our purpose at the moment, to show here, that in the realm of religion, as elsewhere, thought is very powerful, and that it is most important that we should be the masters and not the victims of our thoughts.

12

Desire

These words are being written in the late twentieth century, and at a time when world peace is claimed to be the chief objective of the world's greatest statesmen. Yet the writer has just listened to a radio programme of "world News" which described such a state of unrest in almost every part of the world as to create the impression that another world war is imminent.

Two world wars in half a century, a dozen minor wars, some of which are still going on, and a situation in which one small country is able to "blackmail" the whole world, show us clearly that if a *way of peace* is not soon found, man will rapidly reach the stage when he carries out with his own hands the extinction of the human species.

The development of the most fiendish and destructive weapons has reached such a point that the danger is greater in fact than a mere threat to the human race — it is a threat to the planet on which we live.

This planet Earth, which for millions of years, under the guiding hand of God, has maintained its steady orbit around the sun, is in danger of being blown back by the hand of man into the cloud of cosmic dust from which, at God's command, it first sprang. Peace is not only a desirable state — it has become an urgent necessity. If man and his world are to survive, *a way of peace must be found*.

If we take a look over our shoulders, however, we shall find that this is not a *new* problem. The need may be more urgent than ever before, but the problem is as old as the hills. In the Gospel story of the birth of Jesus, we are told that certain shepherds had a vision of angels filling the sky with their song "Glory to God in the Highest and *on Earth peace*". It is obvious that peace on earth was even then regarded as the most desirable gift one could receive at the hands of God. But peace will not come *as a gift* from God, even though we believe that God desires that state no less than man. Peace will come as a result of man's co-operation with God. "Without God, man cannot — without man, God will not".

No true Christian can fail to be concerned about the fact that world peace seems to be as far away as ever. No true Christian can dare to brush the matter aside as being only the problem of the politician. The matter has gone beyond that; it has become a matter of *intimate concern* for every living soul. Thus, you will see, it is inevitable that any group of *true seekers* must sooner or later turn its attention to this vital matter, and make it a subject for the most earnest and devoted prayer.

Whenever we come face to face with a problem, it is a good thing to examine first of all its causes — if these can be determined, and they usually can. Let us, therefore, see if we cannot dig deeply enough to expose the roots of this great problem of *unrest* which so consistently menaces mankind. Fundamentally, or course, the answer declares itself. *The world is out of harmony* — not merely with itself but with God. But our task is not merely to quote platitudes, but to analyse the reasons for this lack of harmony.

First of all, let us look at the nature of man, for we need to have a deep understanding of the patient before we can hope to treat his disease. We must remember that the human animal began life in the warmth and security of the mother's womb. For many months, "everything was laid on". Every need was met — automatically. There was no threat to its comfort, security or existence.

Then suddenly it is expelled from this "Garden of Eden". The last connecting link with the source of supply of its every need is severed, and a new, tough, and dangerous phase of its existence begins.

Unlike most animals, the human species is not equipped to meet this challenge immediately. It is *utterly dependent* upon others, and particularly upon its mother. Have you ever asked yourself why this should be so? Why the most intelligent of all living creatures should be the most vulnerable of all at birth? It is inconceivable that the Great Designer should be guilty of faulty planning. We must therefore accept the fact that it is *no accident* that determined that the members of the human race should be so "helpless" for the first year or so of their existence.

There is only one acceptable answer to this question, and that is, that a *certain quality* should develop in the species which does not exist in any other. That quality or function is *love*.

If any other animal except the human animal had been as vulnerable at birth, it is a reasonable assumption that by now it would have been as extinct as the Dodo. But the very weakness and dependence of the human child has, instead, welded the race together and developed such qualities as have ensured that the command of God, suggested in the

Book of Genesis, "Go forth and multiply" should be fulfilled.

It is the possession of this quality, more than anything else, that has set man apart, and that shows him to have been shaped "in the image of God". When this quality disappears from the human race the species will die. Is there any connection between this fact and the other fact that, at this present point in history, the human race does indeed stand upon the very brink of annihilation? There must be — and assuredly there is.

During that part of human history which we have on record, there has been a general drift in the direction of losing our great heritage of *love*. That drift has become a landslide during the last century. And this is mainly because man's moral and spiritual development has not kept pace with his mental and material progress.

By his intelligence, man has won for himself a security and comfort enjoyed by no other species, but he has forgotten the basic *law* of nature — God's *law* — that for every privilege there must be a *responsibility*.

No other single factor has had so marked an effect upon the moral quality of the race, as the so-called emancipation of women. It is not suggested that it is necessarily *wrong* that woman should seek to raise her status. She has as much right to do so as any other creature, but we must remember that, as with all other desirable things, *there is always a price to be paid*.

The dependence of a child upon its mother was God's method of developing the vital function of love. In order that *man* should not be just another "toy" or part of a "machine", God gave him complete freedom of choice. He will not "interfere" if we seek to "improve" upon His methods. *But we have no power to frustrate God's purposes. The laws of God cannot be broken* — we can only break ourselves upon those laws. The fundamental *need* of the human race is *love*. There is no substitute for love. If woman can be "emancipated" without danger of frustrating God's plan no harm is done. *But have we been careful enough?*

This brings us to examine this question of *need*, and to compare it with *desire*. In the chapter on Prayer, we had a good deal to say about the dangers of confusing these two terms.

James, the brother of Jesus, gave us an important guide-post when he used the expression *"The Royal Law . . . is love"*. In the fourth chapter of his letter he makes no secret of the fact that in his opinion, *desire* lies at the root of most of the evils upon earth, and particularly the evils of war and fighting. This chapter must be read with care. It will give you a good insight into the dangers of giving rein to our desires.

True need, somewhere or other, has a background of love, and is therefore never on the "wrong" side of God's Laws. For this reason it is always prepared to pay the price. Love is always prepared to sacrifice. *Desire* is the exact opposite. It will often pay a price, when such a price cannot be avoided, but it is usually quite callous about the methods of raising such a price. Need often humbles us, but desire makes us arrogant. Need develops thought and intelligence, but desire is inconsiderate and often quite unintelligent.

James uses the word "lust" more often than "desire", and it is the right word for the purpose. It is unfortunate that down the centuries the word has acquired a slightly different meaning, and is now usually thought of only in connection with sex. James, like many other writers in the New Testament, seems, on the surface, to be obsessed with the idea of "adultery" which, in these days, has no other than a sexual implication. It is safe to say that most of the time the New Testament writers were *not* thinking of sex at all. They had in mind the original meaning of the word — "to alter" (by mixing inferior or impure ingredients with pure). They also very often had in mind the idea of the Church as the "Bride" of Christ, and anything which corrupted it was regarded as adultery.

But, to return to our original thought; the first need of a child is for *love*. This is more urgent even than its need for food. It has ruthlessly been taken from the security and warmth of an environment which it has enjoyed since it became a living entity, therefore the restoration of that sense of all-embracing love is its first need.

This fact is now well known by modern psychologists, and they are aware that one of the chief causes of mental disorder in adults is the complete absence of love during childhood. The psychiatrist will enquire whether his patient was a "breast-fed" or "bottle-fed" baby, not because he is concerned with the nature or quality of the "food", but because he wants to determine the *relationship* between mother and child. A mother who has no alternative but to bottle-feed her child, should be careful to cradle the child lovingly in her arms at feeding times. Many a mother, having no lack of love for her offspring, has nevertheless, done irreparable damage by "propping up" a bottle so that the child can feed while lying in a cot or a perambulator.

In view of the importance of even so small a detail, imagine the impact of the modern way of life, where a mother goes out to work as soon as possible after giving birth to her children. These unfortunate little ones are left to the tender mercies of servants or creche attendants until able to fend for themselves — and then are left to their own devices.

In an age when the toy industry has reached fantastic heights, parents unconsciously attempt to repair the damage by showering gifts upon their children, but the attempt is doomed to failure. The child may acquire, and often does, an insatiable appetite for "things", but his enjoyment is short-lived, and underneath lies an unrecognised *need* which these gifts can never satisfy.

So God made us to be loved, and since love is never a one-sided affair, He also made us to love. This is the primary need of all people — *to love and to be loved*. But down the ages a subtle change has been taking place. As in the case of Cain, man has been offering to God (and to man) a little less than his best. As in the case of the child whose parents have given gifts as a substitute for love, an insatiable desire for more and more gifts is created.

From all this you will see that *desire* can very soon become an evil thing. It is never truly satisfied, and the more it receives, the more its hunger grows. The situation has become so serious in this generation that a man can hardly distinguish any more between his desires and his needs. It is small wonder then, that James and other writers blame *desire* for most of the evils of the world.

With the same deep insight into the fundamentals of life, the Book of Genesis once more pin-points the problem. "I have given you all things", said God, "to satisfy your every *need*. But there is one tree in the garden whose fruit you must not eat". This tree, according to the story, had nothing to do with man's need. If only man had had the good sense to resist *desire*, there might have been a very different story to tell, but once he had given way, he was on the downward path, since his desire could never be fully satisfied.

It goes without saying that desire is the arch enemy of contentment and thus of peace and happiness. This means that we have to go right back to where we started. We know why it is so difficult to achieve world peace — for world peace must begin with individual peace.

In the light of all this, is there anything *you* can do to help to bring about world peace ? There is, of course, and quite obviously the point where you must begin is with your own self. Man cannot change the world until he has learned to change himself.

The best way to develop a contented heart is to have a *thankful* heart. Before desire has a chance to get a grip upon you, first enumerate your many blessings. There is no better advice than the advice given in that old revivalist hymn: "Count your many blessings, name them one by one (that is, dwell upon them) And it will *surprise* you . . ." It certainly will. Not only will it surprise you to see how much you have to be thankful for, but it will also surprise you to see a pattern forming before your eyes — the pattern of your life — piece by piece, falling into place like a great jig-saw puzzle. And finally it will surprise you to find that your desires are drifting away.

As you lay bare to yourself the truth of the way in which God has supplied and *will* continue to supply your every *need*, your desires begin to reveal themselves in all their insignificance, until finally a great contentment fills the place they once held in your life.

The Apostle's answer to this great problem of life was to cultivate a thankful heart. That is why, again and again we read: "In all things giving thanks". Don't ever make the mistake of thinking that God is a vain Being, always hankering after your tributes. He isn't like that at all. The *need* to give thanks is born within our hearts because — *it is our most effective weapon against desire.*

13

The Problem of Suffering

Many Christians are baffled by the presence of so much obvious suffering in a world which is claimed by their religion to be controlled by a *God of love*. To them it seems incredible that a loving God should "allow" so many terrible things to happen.

They are even more disturbed by the apparent injustice of the fact that so often innocent people suffer as a result of the actions of guilty people. It seems to them that very often the good things they do in this life are rewarded by evil, and on the other hand, it is not uncommon to see the most unscrupulous and wicked people apparently profiting by their dishonesty.

First of all it needs to be said that all this only presents a problem to those people who believe in a "good God". To those who do not believe in God at all, there can be no such problem. If the universe is, as one "scientist" or philosopher put it, no more than an "accidental collocation of atoms", then one could hardly expect anything better — the quality of justice could not exist in such a chaotic state.

And to those who prefer to accept the idea of an overall "Intelligence" — utterly impersonal and outside the possibility of human understanding — there is also no problem, for we could not assess the "character" of such a power or even dare to assume that it had such a thing as character in terms that we understand.

It is only when we think of God as the source of all goodness; as the high standard of justice; as One who *loves* us and desires the best for us; as a strong "Father" with a large family of weak children — it is only then that the problem of suffering in the world becomes a matter demanding some acceptable solution.

We need to study this matter very carefully if we are to reach such a solution.

First of all, let us look at the general effect of this apparently uncontrolled distribution of suffering. A few examples will help us. Take the case of a drunken driver who does not have the sense to leave his car behind when he comes home from a gay party. He comes into collision with another car driven by a good, sober, earnest Christian who has spent his life in kindness and consideration for other people. The drunkard is scarcely injured, but the good man is crippled for life, and his wife and children are left to the care of a poor, broken creature, unable to earn the good salary he once enjoyed. Both the once healthy provider and protector and the innocent wife and children are doomed to suffer. No human court of justice can readjust the situation. Whatever punishment is meted out to the drunkard, it will not restore the health and vitality of the victim, and no amount of compensation can give back to the sufferer his strong limbs and perfect health. Ought the "good God" to have allowed such a thing to happen?

Or take the case of a good Christian woman who loves children and would undoubtedly make an excellent mother. Her first child is born a hopeless case of cerebral palsy. The second child is a normal, healthy and lovely child, but is killed through the carelessness of an irresponsible youth on a motor cycle. Her third child is found to have an incurable disease, and lives only for a few short and painful years. Nothing that the mother and father have ever done could deserve such extreme "punishment" — indeed, both were in every sense of the word, *innocent*. How can a God of Love allow such things to happen?

Well, that is the problem. Let us see if there is any alternative. It would appear that there are two possibilities. Firstly, that God could have stopped or prevented these terrible things from happening. But in an earlier chapter of this book we have seen it "proved" that *God does not interfere*. He has made this universe to work by immutable *law*. Any interference with such *law* could only result in such chaos as to make the world an impossible place to live in at all.

The alternative, in the case of the drunken driver, is that God might have "prevented" him from driving on that occasion. But God has given to every one of us a *free will* (a freedom of choice) and He will *not* control our decisions; *He will not use us as mere puppets*, for that would be a reversal of His own plan for mankind.

There seems to be only one other angle of approach. Should God have been more careful in His planning? Should He have been more farsighted and realised the possible effects of the *law* which He made for the control of the universe? Should He not have made a law which says, in effect, that we can only get from this life *those things that we deserve*? On the surface it may appear that this would have been a wiser or at least a "fairer" *law* — one that offered perfect *justice*. Everybody would have been born healthy and happy, and would remain so until they became guilty of doing something that merited punishment. There would have been no risks and no hardships in life unless we were disobedient, and the only fear that would remain would be a fear of our own possible waywardness.

Unfortunately, however, that presents only one side of the matter. In such a world we would also only receive such "good" as we deserved. You would, for instance, no longer be able to drive your motor car. It might be true that you honestly earned the money with which you bought it, but was it *your* brains that designed it? You are utterly dependent upon the endeavours of other people for the petrol which came out of the earth on the other side of the world. The very roads you must use were built by other people, and are the result of some other person's planning and organisation. The small amount of tax that you usually so grudgingly pay could never make such amenities available unless millions of other people were prepared to share co-operatively with you. The good God made the sun to shine upon the just and the unjust alike, and the rain to fall upon the righteous and the unrighteous, but if only the good are to receive these blessings, how can they exist at all? Every good thing we enjoy, from the food we eat and the clothes we wear, to the houses we live in, are the product of other people's efforts and other people's brains and other people's co-operative planning. Not by the most vivid stretch of the imagination could we say that we had either earned or deserved them.

Would you really like to live in a world where you only got what you deserved? Is it not true that we would all prefer to live in the world as it is, with all the risk of undeserved disaster, rather than in a world where we only received the very small benefits that we really earn or deserve?

There is, however, another angle which we ought also to explore. In another chapter we shall speak of "Balance". To every positive there is a negative. All things have their opposite. And when we look at this closely, we shall realise that if there were no such things as "bad", we should not even be able to understand the term "good". If there were no such thing as "cold" we could never appreciate warmth. Light is only meaningful as we contrast it with darkness. Thus we begin to understand that if there were no suffering in the world, we would never understand the meaning of "joy", or experience it.

A world created without the possibility of unpleasant things and unpleasant experiences could have no joy or pleasure. Nor must we overlook the fact of another implication of the *law* of Balance. We cannot get something for nothing in this world. Life's ledger must be balanced. There is always a "price that must be paid". Every privilege must be balanced with a responsibility. Strength can only be bought at the cost of effort. If we had no hardships, and no sufferings, and no temptations in this life, we should also have no character, no strength, no ambition. We should be too weak to survive.

This fact, however, has led to some muddled thinking about the nature of God. There are many people who say: "God sent these things to *try* us," as if God had specially arranged certain tests for us. This is only true in a very general and indirect sense. It is true that God "allowed" the possibility of evil, so that "good" may evolve. God allowed the possibility of suffering so that qualities of endurance may evolve. But it is *not true* that God *sends* any bad thing to any particular person for any particular reason. It is God's will that all His people should be perfect. Sickness, disease, suffering and evil are all as abhorrent to God as "sin". He "permits" them to exist only so that we might be strengthened and ennobled by triumphing over them.

We should therefore regard these things as a challenge to the best that is in us. Almost every worth-while thing in life has come about because some man or some woman has responded to the challenge to overcome some evil thing. Therefore, let us rather be pleased that there is such a thing as suffering in the world, for without it there could be no compassion. Let us be glad that there is such a thing as *need*, for without it there could be no such thing as *love*.

One last thought on the subject is this: we have not yet developed to the stage when we understand the *whole truth* about God's *laws*. If God has allowed suffering, and with it the possibility that the innocent may have to suffer without obvious cause, we can be equally sure that God has made available a means of overcoming *every* disaster. We cannot be tempted beyond our capacity to resist, nor are we called upon to suffer more than we can bear. There is strength available for those who are tuned to receive it. Thousands of years ago, faced with disaster, the great prophet Elisha was able to say to his servant with calm assurance: "The forces that are with us are greater than those that are against us".

14

Healing

The most extraordinary thing about the Bible, and the New Testament in particular, is that it is peculiarly personal. You may read a history, a biography, or an historical novel, and be quite spellbound by its vivid descriptiveness and interest, yet put it down with casual indifference, knowing that it was about other times and other people. It is quite impossible to do this with the Bible. You always feel that it is speaking *to you*. There is always the inescapable consciousness that it is speaking to you personally — that the central message of any passage is for you — *and that it is never out-dated*. The Bible may lack the wealth of descriptiveness of other books, yet its characters spring to life, and its scenes become familiar in a way that leaves you in no doubt that you, *personally*, are involved.

This being the case, it is all the more remarkable that one aspect of the teaching of Jesus has, down the ages, been systematically pushed to one side as if it had little more than an historical interest. This is the Healing Ministry of Jesus.

It is impossible to read the Gospel stories without realising that Jesus was as concerned for the bodies of people as He was for their souls. No other religion shows such concern for the body except, perhaps, Buddhism, and, after all, Buddhism is rather a philosophy than a religion.

From the very beginning of His ministry, Jesus healed and comforted, and when He sent out his disciples on their first mission, His command was to *heal* and to preach. Later, when He sent out seventy it was again to *heal* and to preach, and finally, when He parted from His disciples, His command to them was to "Preach the Gospel (good news) to every creature, *and to heal the sick*".

The disciples had no doubt in this matter. Right from the start, the healing of sick people became part of their ministry. Later, the healing power of Paul was such that people fought for parts of his clothing in the superstitious belief that it might have healing properties. There can be no doubt that the Healing Ministry was a very real and very important feature of the early Church.

When we consider all this evidence, we must ask ourselves the question, if we are honest: "Was Jesus talking to me, or only to His disciples when He said 'Heal the sick'?"

If we admit the possibility of a negative answer to this question, then we must, in reason, admit that every other command may equally have been directed only to others, and this would make nonsense of the whole Gospel of Jesus. If Jesus did not ask you to heal, then He did not ask you to forgive. If He did not command you to have compassion on the sick, then He did not ask you to carry one another's burdens. If He did not promise that you should be able to do even greater works than His own, then He did not promise that your prayers would be answered.

There can be no doubt that when Jesus said "Be ye perfect", He meant perfect in body, mind and spirit. There can be no doubt that He was as concerned for the body as for the soul, and there can be no doubt that when He said: "Heal the sick", He was speaking, not merely to a small body of disciples (pupils), but to every one of us.

If God desires us to be perfect, then it must be a fact that sickness and disease are as much an offence to Him as sin. It is useless to imagine that we can win God's favour by presenting to Him a spotless soul if, in the process of achieving this state, we neglect, or have no concern for our bodies.

But there is more to it than that. Man is not three creatures — body, mind and soul. He is one entity — one *person*. If any part is sick, then the whole is sick. We cannot cut ourselves off from mind and body and present to God a sinless soul. His command is to be *perfect*, and we must therefore strive to be perfect in every part of our being. If we are sick, we are *out of harmony*, and we have a duty to get well.

Up to this point we have been considering our own souls and our own bodies, but Jesus made it very clear that we have a much greater responsibility than this. We have a duty to our neighbours too. All too often, as Christians, we concern ourselves with the morals of our neighbours — we feel that we have a duty to care for their souls and to lead them to what we call (rather loosely) "salvation". Very often we go even further and try, as we believe, to improve their minds. But for some reason we fight shy of being actively concerned about their health. We will run errands, provide comforts, take flowers— but the rest, we feel, is the province of the specialists, the doctors. We may be sympathetic; we may be compassionate; but we do not feel *responsible*.

It is true that the Christian Church has been responsible for great work centred upon the relief of sickness. It has inspired and supported the work of building hospitals and clinics and health centres. It is true that the Church has been behind most of the social organisations concerned with the care of cripples, lepers, the blind and the deaf and dumb, and with the comfort of the aged and infirm. It is also true that most Christians support these organisations with their gifts of money and service. And all this is for the good of humanity and the alleviation of suffering. But the important thing is that Christians in general do *not* feel a *personal responsibility*. Their participation is remote and detached.

Within the Church itself, concern for the sick rarely goes further than to "take it to the Lord in prayer". What cannot be taken care of by doctors and nurses (the professionals) we hand over to God with the comfortable and pious feeling that we have done all that can be expected of us.

This is not quite good enough. Indeed, in the humble opinion of the writer, it is rather shirking the real issue. In the same way that, if a man is sick in body, he is sick all over — so, if one man is sick, *humanity* is sick. We are all part of a greater whole. If any part of our body is sick it is a matter of concern for the whole body. And if any part of the human race is sick, then it must be the concern of the whole race. Cain tried to dodge the issue when he said: "Am I my brother's keeper?" But Jesus gave the final answer when He told the story of "The Good Samaritan". If your neighbour is sick, *it is your business*. We cannot escape the fact that God calls us to this work.

If you examine this situation carefully and honestly, you will see that a clear pattern emerges. We have two outstanding duties. One is to be perfect in body, mind and soul, and the other is to help our neighbour to a like perfection.

Nevertheless, Jesus told us that before we can take the speck of dust out of our neighbour's eye, we must first remove the plank from our own. It is clear, beyond argument, that we should make every effort to achieve true harmony in our own lives so as to be fit enough to help our neighbour also to come into perfect harmony with God. Let us, therefore, first of all see what steps we can take for the perfection of our own personal health.

In an earlier chapter we have tried to show that God created us with a perfect "built in" system of self help. The body is equipped with every weapon needed to fight against the intrusion of disease, or to heal any part of the body which may have become infected.

Unfortunately, we have, for so many years, neglected to use these facilities fully, so that we no longer have perfect command of them and therefore cannot always bring them into action to heal ourselves. We are literally forced to call upon the help of trained doctors. Our first duty is to begin to redevelop our own powers, using the great help which is always available in *prayer*. Let our aim indeed be to become "perfect" in the sense of being independent of outside help. Medical assistance is not to be despised, and it may be some considerable time before we can become independent of it, but this should be our goal and there are certain steps which we can take at once which will help tremendously in this direction.

The first step is to get rid of superstition. There are millions of people who would claim that they are not superstitious, but few could survive a careful test on this subject. Most of us have deep-rooted convictions about certain things, particularly with regard to health, which more often than not are *sheer superstition*. Get rid of them and begin to use your own brains and your faith in the good judgement of God. You were intended to be healthy and your body contains all the equipment necessary to make and keep you so. Believe this above all things.

The second step is a very logical one and should need no stressing. *Do not abuse your body.* This is only another way of saying *use your body with care*. It is a finely tuned machine of infinite potential and fantastic durability, but, like every other machine, it has its limits. Do not overload it. It may here be of help for us to look at some of the common abuses to which the body is so often exposed, so that we may be able to avoid them.

(1) *Over-eating*. The true function of eating is to supply fuel to the body sufficient for its normal requirements. Any excess is an overload. It is unfortunate that today, feeding has become a matter of enjoyment or pleasure rather than a necessity, and in consequence, most people eat more than is necessary, and a good deal which has no particular value as fuel. The body tends to store what it cannot consume, and the effect is rather like adding more and more trucks to a goods train without adding any pulling power to the engine. The engine is called upon to do more work than it was built for, and sooner or later will crack under the strain.

It is an unfortunate feature of modern life that we no longer correctly interpret the body's signals. We think we are "hungry" when in fact we have a "desire" — not a need — for enjoyable food or snacks and sweetmeats. Learn to interpret your signals correctly and do not think you can eat indiscriminately and then put matters right by adopting some special diet for a short period. The true answer is not diet but mastery of your desires.

(2) *Under-eating.* It is equally important not to eat less than is necessary. There are many people who are guilty of this fault, and though it may be true that it is less dangerous than over-eating, it still puts an unnecessary strain upon certain organs of the body.

People have many "fads" about eating, and vast numbers (especially among women) *never* eat breakfast. They "just don't feel like it", so they set out upon a day's work, forcing the heart to draw heavily on every reserve of fuel to keep going. To eat only when it is a matter of "enjoyment" is an abuse of the system only a little less than over-eating. Certain light foods, particularly the cereals and milk can provide the necessary energy to begin the day's work. It isn't necessary to "stoke up" with bacon and eggs, steak, fish or any other heavy meal.

(3) *Avoid tension.* Coronary thrombosis and other similar heart complaints have become the scourge of the twentieth century, and the reason for it is the tension under which far too many people live. Many people have forgotten how to relax. This tension can be seen in the faces of the people whom you pass in the street. It is true, of course, that the conditions under which people live and work in these crowded busy days are a contributory factor, but it is wrong to attempt to put all the blame there. There never was a time when people worked fewer hours in a week. There never was a time when they had so many aids to comfort and relaxation. There never was a time when it was so easy to share responsibility. The real reason for the tension springs from a more subtle source.

There is more suspicion and less trust among people. It seems that every person is involved in competition. Not the healthy competition of sport, but the fight for survival. This state of mind is reflected in the attitude of people to their dress, their homes, their occupations, their children and even their games. Organised sport is no longer fun — it is deadly warfare. The team spirit has almost disappeared in an age of specialisation, and brotherly love has become the most unusual attribute of humanity. Laughter is forced and unreal and many people have almost forgotten how to smile. The joke most likely to bring forth a laugh in these days is usually one which involves the downfall or discomfiture of some other person.

Since it is God's purpose that men shall live together in peace and love, it is inevitable that any set of circumstances which conspires against such a condition *must be against His law*, and therefore involves the gravest danger to survival. We cannot break God's Laws — we can only break *ourselves* upon them. Therefore it must be our aim as far as in us lies, to rectify, first in ourselves, and then in our neighbour, this unfortunate state of mind which militates against health and happiness.

There is a formula. Since we can only live one day at a time, let us resolve to live that day as if life itself depended upon it. Jesus said: "Sufficient for the day is the evil thereof". He meant just what He said. We have enough evil to contend with in any one day, and it is wrong and dangerous to concern ourselves either with the days that are past, or the problems of a doubtful tomorrow. Let us then see how we can improve *today*.

Begin with a smile. If you have nothing particularly to smile about, force yourself to think about something pleasant. Then begin to enumerate your many blessings. Think of the ways in which your day is likely to be much better than the day of so many unfortunate people on this earth. Resolve to make this a happy day by making someone else — anyone — a little happier. Refuse to entertain a negative or unhappy thought. Go to an open window and breathe deeply of the life-giving air and thank God that you can breathe it. Through all the day smile as often as possible and refuse to frown. Eat enough but not too much and thank God—not perfunctorily (as so many do when saying "grace") but sincerely — for making the food available. Be on your guard. At the first sign of anger, breathe deeply and slowly, and remember that other people can only hurt you as much as you are willing to allow them. Do not give them the pleasure of seeing your anger rise, and knowing that they have scored a hit. If problems arise, do not panic. Slowly consider the situation; do all you can to resolve the matter, and mentally but earnestly hand over the rest to God. Then, since you can do no more, *put it out of your mind*. If the world comes to an end — you could not have prevented it anyway.

Remember that no situation is ever improved by getting tense, but you yourself become less capable of dealing with it. It may help you to write out the following affirmation, and to stick it to the mirror in your bedroom, where you can read it at the beginning of every day.

God gave me this day. Therefore He wants me to live this day for Him. With His power within me, I cannot fail. If every other friend should foresake me, He will not, and therefore I will be happy this day.

(4) *Refuse to worry.* Stomach disorders, ulcers, and kindred ailments are born of worry, a thing that kills more people than over-work has ever done. It is pointless to say: "I can't help worrying", though most people say just that. *But it is not true.* It may be difficult but it is certainly not impossible. Worry is the most irrational act of which the human animal is guilty. It is destructive in its effects and it is utterly futile because it cannot solve or even relieve a single situation. It is a complete dissipation of energy without a single redeeming feature.

If a difficult situation crops up, *deal with it.* Don't worry about it. Face squarely up to the matter and ask yourself the question: "What steps can I take *at once* to deal with the situation?" Then act at once upon the answer. Next, ask yourself the question: "What plans must be set in motion for the future," and begin to work upon them as soon as they form in your mind. For the rest, having done all that *you* can, you are dependent upon help from some other source. The only sure and reliable source of power is God. Hand the matter over to Him, *and trust Him completely.* To continue to worry is to admit a lack of confidence in God. *You have His promise* — if you do not believe Him then *you have no God.* This sounds terribly final, but it is the plain truth. If you cannot trust God, neither this book nor any other can help you to life and happiness.

(5) *Get rid of bitterness.* Jesus made it abundantly clear to us that we should forgive all those who do us an injury. Peter once raised the question: "What of those who hurt us again and again?" But Jesus was adamant. Even seventy time seven was not to be the limit of our forgiveness. There was a reason for that, and that reason concerns our health.

When we do *not* forgive our enemies, our natural resentment turns to bitterness, and that bitterness causes a malfunction of the glands which feed lubrication to many joints in our bodies. Serious dis-ease is the ultimate result. Have you never wondered why we commonly use the word "bitter" to describe an emotion when in fact it is an adjective describing a "taste"? The reason is that we do in fact become bitter because we have begun to manufacture acids within our bodies in larger quantities than those bodies can use, and thus we do ourselves serious injury.

It is useless to take "acid-free" diets, or antacid medicines while we continue to manufacture unwanted acids within ourselves. There are many so-called organic diseases as well as mental disorders which have their roots in our failure to forgive our enemies, and not least among them are arthritis, gout, rheumatism, gall stones and kindred complaints.

Above all things, we must fight down the desire to "get our own back" — to avenge ourselves. But we must *not* make the mistake of merely "burying" our resentment. *We must truly forgive.* Jesus said that until we can forgive others, we cannot ourselves be forgiven for our faults and failings. But it must be a true and complete forgiveness, or otherwise our resentment will continue to ferment in the depths of our unconscious minds. All this leads us to another step which must also be taken for our health's sake.

(6) *We must get rid of our guilt.* It is not merely our modern psychologists who have recognised the part that guilt plays in our sickness. Jesus pin-pointed it nearly two thousand years ago. Often, when He was healing the sick, He used a different formula from the usual "rise up and walk". He would occasionally say: "Your sins are forgiven". The result was the same — the sickness was cured.

To carry guilt around with us is to throw the whole of our self-healing apparatus out of gear. We become victims of a long list of diseases because we have lost the ability to resist or heal ourselves.

But we have no need to carry our guilt around. We have only to acknowledge our faults to God and He will forgive (wipe them out). Once we have accepted God's forgiveness, our past faults have no power to hurt us. But we must be quite sure that we *have accepted* His forgiveness. Many people fail to accept this greatest of God's gifts — even though it is so freely given. Day after day and night after night they will continue to plead with God for forgiveness of the same old sins, as if God were reluctant to forgive, or that there were no permanence in His forgiveness. It is almost like taking a perverted pride in our own sin, and parading it before God as often as possible. You must understand that this practice is very dangerous to our health. It is not *real* prayer, and therefore there is no *real* forgiveness — not because God is unwilling, but because His forgiveness has obviously *not been accepted.*

True, we must confess our sin, but once we have asked for forgiveness we must *know* that the slate has, as it were, been wiped clean. From that moment we must put the whole business right out of our minds. This is the only way to destroy the power of guilt. Remember, however, that this forgiveness is only possible to us (by reason of God's immutable *law*) when we are equally willing to forgive others — and when we put such willingness into action.

Finally — though it ought not to be necessary to mention this step — *we must avoid all forms of excess.* Many things are quite harmless until indulged in to excess. Moderation in all things is not only a desirable virtue, but it is a great aid to perfect health. The secret lies in the fact that the human body is a most finely balanced "machine". Perhaps the most wonderful in creation. Excess in any direction creates an "imbalance" which leads to malfunction.

These are not the only steps that we can take for our own health. There are many more which will occur to you, such as deep breathing, regular exercise and regular sleep. The thing to do is to take every step towards perfect health, while avoiding "fads" which are no more than sheer superstition.

If we have taken every step to ensure the health of our own bodies, we have already gone a long way towards helping our neighbour, since the best thing we can do is to set a perfect example.

There are some people in this life who seem to *radiate* health and happiness. All who come into contact with them feel uplifted (temporarily at least). The word radiate is well chosen. That is exactly what happens. Thought forms go forth from us like rays, and if all our thought forms are wholesome and healthy and happy, we shall affect every person with whom we come into contact, in a way that can only be for their good.

It is equally true that if our thought forms are negative and unhealthy, we shall spread gloom and unhappiness and even sickness, just as certainly as if we carried active bacteria around with us. Our first step, therefore, in healing our neighbours, is to set a good example by being perfectly well in our own bodies. And the second is to send out nothing but wholesome and positive thoughts.

Never discuss sickness or disease or symptoms with them, and if, as is more than likely, they are the kind of people who delight in discussing their latest "operation" or their present symptoms, do your best to discourage this line of conversation by changing it to any other topic. The third step is to *pray* for them. Do not make the mistake of praying for too many at one time, or your prayer is likely to become no more than a matter of words. It must begin with genuine concern and compassion. You must make it a vivid personal matter, and as you pray, see yourself taking that neighbour by the hand to

Jesus for healing. Do not cease until you see a clear picture in your mind of that neighbour duly healed and fully recovered.

You will be surprised at the powerful results of this method. However, a little note of warning must be sounded. Do not rush around telling all your friends of the wonderful way in which your prayers have been answered and your neighbours healed. To do so is to bolster your own pride, and this will undermine the nobility of character which is developing in your life. *You are being used.* You are a part of *the Body of Christ* — one of His active limbs. Let your reward be the inward joy of having served *Him*. There is no need to tell others, indeed, you will find that the oftener you boast of results, even though you qualify your boasting by verbally giving all the credit to Jesus, the less will be your power, and the less you will have to boast about.

The fourth step is the "Laying on of hands", and this needs careful explanation. The New Testament frequently emphasises the virtue of laying on hands in cases of sickness. But not every person can do this without an uncomfortable feeling that they are open to suspicion. A minister, a deacon or official of the Church may perform the act without arousing any comment, but the average layman or woman does not usually feel the same sense of freedom or privilege. Nevertheless it is a matter of importance *because your body is a conductor*, and to have the best possible chance of success you *must* make a physical contact.

Many people know this instinctively, and so it is that a mother or a nurse will place a hand upon a fevered brow — will kiss an injured finger, or in a hundred ways contrive to "touch" the affected part of the child or person to whom they are trying to minister. Thus you will find a way, without drawing attention to what you really have in mind, of making a *physical contact*. If, for instance, you visit a friend or neighbour in hospital, when you pray with them be sure to take the hand of the patient and hold it all the while you are praying. Or if the patient is very ill, perhaps even unconscious, place your hand upon his or her brow while you are praying. This physical contact will ensure that the healthy power of your own body is transmitted, but even more than this, you become the link through which the power of God may act. The person for whom the prayer is offered will almost always regard you, for the time being at least, as an agent — closely in touch with God, and will always react more positively when linked to God by the touch of your hand.

The next step is a corporate one. Link up with other friends who share your own convictions and your own concern. Join a Prayer Circle or even *start* a Prayer Circle, and meet regularly to commune with God and to pray for the sick. Just as a rope is stronger than a single cord, and a cord stronger than a single thread, so a group of like-minded people praying together commands greater power than a single person praying alone. Also, as the Apostle put it, such a group will *"build each other up"*.

This work of prayer and healing is the Church in action. It has no organisation, no hierarchy, no formality, but it works like the yeast in Jesus' own illustration. There is no greater service that you can offer to humanity. There is no greater challenge to the reality of your Christian experience.

15

Righteousness and Sin

There are two words which occupy a great deal of thought in any religious gathering. They are Righteousness and Sin. Most Christian Churches in this century (as also in the last) seem almost obsessed with the idea of *sin*, and it is certain that almost all of them have their attention focused mainly upon two thoughts — the Righteousness of God and the Sinfulness of man.

The later chapters of the Second Book of Kings comprise a sort of synopsis of the history of Israel, and each generation seems to be classified under one of two headings: "The king (and his people) did that which was right in the sight of God" or "The king (and his people) *sinned* against God".

John the Baptist, the forerunner of Christ, roundly condemned his own generation and called upon the people to "repent" that they might be "saved".

It appears that every Sect or Denomination of the Christian Church begins at the same point — *with the natural assumption that man is sinful* and must be *saved from the consequences of his sin*. The various writers of the Letters in the New Testament carry something of the same message, though often in a less pointed way.

The true seeker is literally bound to consider all the implications of this evidence, and to do so he must come to a better understanding of what is meant by the terms "Righteousness" and "Sin". The first should not present us with much difficulty.

Let us begin with the assumption that we have accepted two important facts. First, that there *is* a God, and second, that God has a personal interest in humanity. If we have not accepted these facts, there is no point at all in considering the questions of righteousness and sin at all, for they would have no meaning.

The God who created us is *obviously* the only One with the authority to set a standard. And, just as obviously, there can be no higher standard than that of His own character. God's purpose for mankind is made clear in the Book of Genesis where we read that God created man in

His own "image". Thus we can say that God desires us to be "*like
Him*". That, and that only, can be *righteousness*. We might, perhaps,
more correctly express this state as "*being right with God*".

In any large precision engineering works, every article must be
made to a certain standard. The articles are checked at various points
in the production process with "gauges" which have been made with
the utmost degree of accuracy. Failure to satisfy the demands of the
gauge leads to "rejection", and the articles falling short must either be
"corrected" or, where this is not practicable, "*scrapped*". If we may use
this as an illustration, it would seem that the human race might well
be treated in the same manner.

In the earliest stages of its development, the only guide (or gauge)
that the human race had consisted of its ability to understand, or to
be able to communicate directly with, the *creator*. Surely the writers
of Genesis had in mind that stage of evolution when man's intelligence
had not yet developed to the point when it could *reason*. Utter reliance
upon God only seemed to dwindle as man became more and more able
to fend for himself. Surely that is what was meant by the references to
"eating of the tree of Knowledge!"

Later, it became necessary for man to be provided with a "written"
specification, as it were, and thus the "Ten Commandments" were
provided. For a while this worked with a moderate degree of success,
but all too soon it became obvious that the mind of man had become
"clever" enough to find loopholes in any "code of laws" and a more
perfect type of "gauge" became necessary. This "pattern", if we may
call it so, runs like a golden thread through the whole of the Old Testament until, finally, after the gap between the Old Testament and the
New, we see the "gauge" provided in the person of Jesus. It was no
accident that the Name given to Him was "Immanuel", for this word
means, literally, "God with us" — and this is a perfect expression of
His *function*.

Broadly speaking, this is the view (though not often expressed in
this manner) which is held by the "Christian" or Christianised people
of the world today. Unfortunately it leaves out of account certain
factors that have a large influence upon the character and way of life
of most people in the world today. One of the most important factors
is that God created man with a most remarkable "memory" — and
that that memory is "collective".

In a normal healthy state, a person's memory is all-embracing and
of almost infinite capacity. When we say that we cannot remember a

certain thing, we really mean that we are temporarily unable to bring that thing to the surface of our conscious mind. In actual fact there is *nothing* that is completely forgotten. Everything that we see or hear or experience is inexorably entered in the "files" of our memories. This memory might be likened to a computor of infinite capacity. Every sound; every sight; every "feeling", is fed into this computor, which in any normal healthy person becomes an almost infallible mine of information.

All our instinctive or "unconscious" acts are regulated by this computor which works at lightning speed. Let us look at a small illustration of how this works. Suppose you desire to rise from your chair and walk across the room. Your conscious mind concerns itself only with the decision to do so, and with the reasons for that decision. It does not concern itself with the mechanics of the operation. *Yet you cannot* rise from that chair without bringing into play a whole series of nerves and muscles, which, in turn, can only operate on very specific information fed to them from the "computor".

On your decision to act, an order is automatically fed into this computor which takes over and provides all the necessary data to operate the various part of the bodily "machine" and to complete the complex process of moving the whole body to the place desired. It must, for instance, know the exact weight of the body (though *you* may not be consciously aware of that figure) before it can cause the muscles to produce the necessary amount of energy required to raise it. It must be informed as to where the "centre of gravity" is located (though you are not consciously able to provide the information). Without this vital information there would be no sense of balance and walking would be impossible.

Certain conditions can seriously disrupt this orderly process. For instance, an excess of alcohol in the bloodstream can temporarily upset the efficiency of the computor so that the correct orders do not reach the nerve terminals. Walking now becomes difficult because the necessary information regarding the centre of gravity and the exact weight is not regulating the muscle impulses.

Again, if false information is fed to the computor, *it cannot give the right answer*. This important fact is easily verified by carrying out a simple experiment. I have walked into a room carrying an empty suit case in such a manner as to convey the idea that it was extremely heavy. Gasping for breath I have placed it on the floor with evident relief. Completely deceived by this performance, my friend in the room has come forward to my assistance. Although no word has been spoken, certain false information has been fed into my friend's "computor". In order to move the suit case he puts forth an enormous excess of effort with the result that he falls over backwards.

We shall return to this interesting discussion later in this book, because it has so great an influence upon almost every aspect of our living, but for the moment enough has been said to prove that we are *not* always entirely responsible (consciously) for our actions. Those who, in these modern days, have had any experience of man-made computors, will know that they can only give correct answers if fed with accurate data.

Now most of our memory is based upon facts (experiences), but *not all of it*. Especially during our childhood, a great deal goes into our memory files which is not based upon our *own* experiences, but upon what we are *told* or *taught* by parents and teachers. This information is "second-hand" and is therefore not always reliable. It is not difficult, therefore, for you to see how great an influence upon our characters other people can have. While we are young we are very definitely at the mercy of parents, teachers, ministers and others who have the power to "mould" our characters — either deliberately or accidentally. I have heard the boast by a Roman Catholic priest: "Give me your child until it is seven years old and *it will always be a Catholic*". Without going too deeply into the significance of all this, let us take a quick look at the question of how this can affect us in the realm of religion.

From the earliest age a child may be told that there is a God, and that certain things please that God while others displease Him. This "knowledge" is fed into the youthful brain just like any other sound, sight or experience, and it will be used *instinctively* at some later date. When, at some stage in later life, the person asks his mind *for the first time:* "Who created the world? — Who made life?" his conditioned computor will immediately supply an answer, but the answer supplied will not truly be the result of *reasoning* — it will have been based upon second-hand information. *It will not be the result of personal experience.*

It must be obvious to you that when this sort of thing has been happening for generation after generation, vast numbers of people begin life with ideas of religion which can be very far removed from the truth and certainly have little bearing upon personal experience.

In consequence, only very few people truly *seek* for God. Most of the others think that they *know*, and act accordingly.

One of the results of all this is that every person has what we loosely call a *conscience*, and this, quite erroneously, has come to be considered as *"the voice of God within"*. It is nothing of the kind. In reality it is very largely the voice of other people's experience. The superstitions and the "hoodoos" of generations of humans have gradually been built into the minds of people, and have a profound effect upon their thought and behaviour.

By the time of the coming of Jesus into the world, there was virtually no longer any direct communication with God. Even the few enlightened ones who, for centuries, had tried to correct the downward moral trend — the prophets — seemed to have come to an end, and the gauge of the *law* (the Law of Moses) had become distorted until it was no longer a true expression of the Righteousness of God.

Into this setting Jesus came to bring back religious sanity. He began the great work of *atonement* (at-one-ment). Cleansing the slate, as it were, so that men might be brought back into *harmony* with God. If you can disentangle the truth about Jesus from all the accretions of over nineteen centuries, you will have the perfect pattern against which to test your own righteousness — your rightness with God.

But Jesus, whose knowledge of human nature was deeper than that of anyone the world had ever known, knew exactly what would happen as the years passed by. He knew that even the disciples could not be relied upon to *remember* all He had taught them, and hearsay is never a true substitute for *experience*.

He did all that He could, even at the cost of His life — for the laying down of His life was in accordance with the "built in" convictions of that age, to sponge clean the tablets of their minds. *And then he taught them to seek a real and personal experience.* The few words that have survived to teach us this truth need no interpreting to have the right impact upon us: "Tarry here until ye receive power from on high". But if you have read the earlier chapters of this book, you will have no difficulty in realising that this was but another way of saying: *"Wait upon God* until you *experience* His Presence". This, and this alone is the way to come into harmony with God. Here, and only here, will you know and understand what is meant by *righteousness*.

And all this leads us to seek the truth about the opposite of righteousness — the truth about sin. There can be only one satisfactory definition of sin. It is anything which we voluntarily or deliberately do which destroys our perfect harmony with God — anything in fact, which is calculated to bring about a *separation* from Him.

It is quite useless to draw up a list or "code" of things which may be considered to be "sins". Man has been trying to do just that right down the ages. It was happening long before the advent of Moses, though it found its crystallisation in the Tablets of the Law. And it is still happening today. We have seen how rapidly ten simple guides were transformed into hundreds of petty rules and regulations — the Books of Leviticus and Deuteronomy are full of them — and we have seen how worthless this method had become by the time Jesus arrived upon the human scene. But few people pause to consider that this process started all over again, even before the last of the disciples had passed to his reward.

The simple Gospel of Jesus was reduced, in His last sermon, to a single, straightforward, glorious and all-embracing *commandment*. "That ye love one another, even as I have loved you". And it was on that single note that the early Church came into being. But before fifty years had passed — and we see this clearly in the unfolding story of the rest of the New Testament — a new code of laws, not very different from the "Old Covenant" was already in being. And today, after nearly two thousand years, the list of rules and regulations is as long and as elaborate as any that the Hebrew people ever knew.

The emphasis of the Church is always upon *sin*, and how to save people from its deadly influence, and this would be well enough if the Church still knew what it was talking about — if only it had not confused sin and righteousness with "crime" and "codes" of rules.

Vast numbers of people in this age, though they accept the idea of God, reject the Church because it appears to offer them *no answer* to life's problems. And equally vast numbers who remain within the Church, because they can find no other answer, are still in the grip of that thing called conscience which gives them no relief, and leaves them continually groping in the dark.

They read in the Bible and they are taught by their clergy that Jesus came to bring "salvation" (from the bondage of sin), yet they do not experience the sense of release which ought to be theirs. They could not say in sincerity that they have been "set free" or that they have experienced the "fullness of life" promised by Jesus, or that they are filled with "the Holy Spirit".

To some there comes a smug self-satisfaction that they are "not as other men are" — a type recognised by Jesus — but all that they really have is a veneer of piety. To others, an ever deepening consciousness of their own "sin" and a constant fight against temptation is the only reward. This leads to a continual state of introspection, where every thought and act must be closely examined and tested against certain accepted standards, with the inevitable result of an unconscious "selfishness" which is the very opposite of true Christianity.

There are a few, mostly to be found among the newer "Sects" where a short-lived excitement is experienced, and the people concerned will for a while be transformed and even filled with a kind of joy or exultation. On close analysis this appears to be no more than a subtle form of "hysteria" and all too soon wears off.

There are others again who translate their earnest desire into enthusiastic action. They throw themselves into all sorts of vigorous crusades and campaigns for the extension of the Church; for the protection of the weak; for the emancipation of the oppressed; for the abolition of every form of so-called evil and the salvation of "sinners". These, perhaps, get more out of their religion than many, for the simple reason that they put more into it, but the trained psychologist would recognise most of this as a form of "rationalisation".

The truth of the matter is that all these people are under the tyranny of this thing called conscience. Their sense of what is right and what is wrong does not come from inward knowledge (born of experience) of what God *is*, but as the result of a "conditioned" mind — the product of other people's teachings and fears. This was what Jesus was driving at when He made two profoundly important statements. First, that "the *truth* shall make you *free*". Free from the bondage of a conditioned mind and an artificial conscience. And second, "Ye must be born again" by which He meant that you must start all over again — free from the influence of all the built in hoodoos and prejudices which warp your judgement and cloud your vision. He even carried the thought into the prayer that He gave us — "Deliver us from evil". And the evil He had in mind was that which is already built into the mind — the guilt complexes; the inferiority complexes, and other disabling factors which are born of heredity and environment.

The first essential to a real understanding of sin and righteousness, is to *make true contact with God*. This may come in a blinding flash of inspiration in some emotional moment — even, perhaps, after listening to some unusual sermon. More often it comes as a result of earnest *seeking*. But when it comes, however it may come, *cling to it with all your might*. Follow no man's advice — no man's teaching. Check it all against the *character of Jesus*, and not what you have *heard* or *read* about His teachings. You will *know* that you have found God, and you

cannot *sin* unless you deliberately decide to *set him aside*. Don't even
trust your conscience until you are quite sure that all the old accretions
have been washed away.

The effect of thousands of years of wrong teachings has been to
create the idea of God watching over humanity with an all-seeing eye,
and very critically observing every detail of man's thoughts and actions,
and entering the results into some vast Book of Judgement. Some
sections of the Church openly preach of a "Day of Judgement" when
a reckoning is made and rewards and punishments duly meted out.
Others hold fast to the idea of "eternal damnation" and even the threat
of "hell fire".

It is impossible to equate these two last ideas with the belief or
knowledge that God is *love*. This is a doctrine of *fear*, and its effects
cannot fail to be utterly destructive. Until these ideas are utterly
expunged from the mind, there can be no possibility of harmony with
God, and the full flower of man's true potential can never bloom.

It is necessary that we should now turn our thoughts to the idea of
the rewards of righteousness and the punishments of sin.

16

By Their Fruits

A close examination of the records that we have of the teachings of Jesus cannot fail to reveal His thoughts on the natural consequences of our human behaviour. On one occasion He put it plainly into words: "Whatsoever a man sows, that shall he also reap". And no amount of juggling with the theme of "saved by the blood of Jesus" will blot out the significance of this statement.

It may well be that wishful thinking has been behind a great deal of the utterly mistaken teaching that Jesus "took upon Himself the *punishment* for our sin". Or (and this is only putting the same proposition in another way) that by the magic of "calling upon His Name", we can be reprieved. Such a conception makes a mockery of the whole principle of *justice*. That a God of *love* should make His own perfect Son a scapegoat for all the evil in the world is too ludicrous to merit a moment's consideration.

No rationally minded seeker can fail to realise that, somewhere along the line, there has been a complete misunderstanding of the idea of "Redemption".

We know that Jesus did not die for *nothing*. To remove the Cross from the heart of Christianity would be to destroy our religion altogether but it is necessary that we should understand clearly what part the crucifixion played in God's plan for the redemption of the world. It is deadly dangerous to continue in the belief that the sacrifice of Jesus can bring us immunity from the consequences of sin.

Some of the old teachings, and in particular, some of the old revivalist hymns are very misleading. "Washed in the blood of the Lamb" and "All my sins on Jesus laid", and similar expressions have led to the belief that our guilt has been transferred to Jesus, and that, in some magic way, we are no longer responsible. *Nothing could be further from the truth.* By the very nature of things *guilt is never transferable.*

Part of all this confusion is due to that old failure to understand fully the nature of *sin*. There is, in fact, *no such thing as a sin*. There is only a sinful person. When a person has committed an act which is opposed

91

to God's *laws*, we say he has *sinned*. But this universe which God has created is controlled, not be a continuous series of independent decisions, *but by the immutable law of cause and effect*. Every act, good or bad; right or wrong, has its consequence. Having been *done* it cannot be *undone*. It is true that damage can be "repaired", but an *act* cannot, as it were, be *"un-acted"*.

This leads us to take a closer look at the whole question — so let us, for the moment, look at it from a purely *human* point of view. This may help us to achieve a clearer understanding of the situation.

Let us suppose that a man breaks a "law", that is, he commits a "crime". Two things arise from this. First, there is the *consequence* of his crime. This is inevitable. If he kills a man — someone is dead. If he steals money — someone is the poorer. If he heaves a brick through a shop window — the glass is broken and so on.

The criminal may appear on the surface, to be untouched by the consequences of his act. It may even seem at times that he has escaped them altogether (though, as will be shown, he never does). But the second thing to consider is that there is usually a *penalty* to be paid for committing the crime.

If and when the "criminal" is brought to judgement, the judge may be harsh, or he may be lenient. In certain instances he may even remit the penalty altogether. Or, in a case where a "fine" is imposed as the punishment, a third party may be allowed to pay it. In other words, the "penalty" and *not the consequences* may be remitted. You may be *"forgiven"* but the consequences remain.

Let us put this in the form of a story—this was, after all, the method of Jesus. A father has a ne'er-do-well son, whom, in spite of all his faults, he still loves very dearly. A time comes when the boy commits an act which brings shame on his family and disgrace upon his father. The matter *must* be dealt with, and so the father confronts the erring son. "What you have done is so bad", he says, "that I ought to throw you out of the home and disown you. However, in spite of all your faults, you are still my son and I love you too much to do this, so I am going to give you the thrashing of your life in the hope that it will teach you a lesson, *but I will not cast you away*".

The *consequences* were that a father *was* disgraced (nothing could undo this) and the boy paid a price, *but the penalty* of being cast off was remitted.

Assuming that every other consequence of sin could somehow be avoided, there is one that cannot, for every thought and act causes a subtle change in the cells of the brain. Everything is registered. When you have done wrong, you are never quite the same person again. And one of the important effects of this is that each "sin" makes it more and more easy to sin again, and more and more difficult to tell right from wrong. This is an inescapable consequence.

This begins to show itself in your general character, until even other people can recognise it. Thus your whole way of life becomes "conditioned". This was what Jesus was referring to when He spoke of a "tree being recognised by its fruits".

The *penalty* would be, ultimately, that you have shut yourself outside the family of God. Not that God has "cast you off", but that *you* have "walked out" on Him. You would have drifted so far away as never to be able to recognise His voice, or ever, by your own efforts, to be able to come into harmony with Him again. *This is where Jesus comes in.* Forgiveness *is* possible. The final *penalty* can be remitted. This is the *hope* at the heart of Christianity.

However, we must not lose sight of a very important fact. True salvation is not just a matter of hope. We *must* come at last into harmony with God. The death of Jesus on the Cross does not magically transform us into something we were not. It has given us the hope that, in spite of what we *have been*, we will not be shut off from God for ever. *There is always a chance for us.* But it gives us more than that, otherwise we would still be left in the position of having to rise by our own efforts *alone*. And this we *could not* do. This would be rather like trying to lift ourselves from the ground by tugging upon our own shoe laces. We cannot save ourselves.

The true significance of the Cross lies in the fact that Jesus submitted, not merely to the pain of a cruel death — many others have selflessly done as much as that — but to something that goes much deeper. He who had, by His perfect and spotless life, earned the reward of inheriting a place in the "highest heaven" (we shall discuss this later) *pledged himself* to remain *accessible* to every man — until every man was perfected. Liberated from the "bondage of the flesh" *He could now do this.*

Do you see the significance of this fact? Jesus remains timelessly engaged in the business of saving men's souls, when He could have been released from all such toil and agony. He continues to share our lives, our pains, our frustrations, our sorrows and our temptations, until we are *saved* — when He could have been enjoying His rightful place (as the Bible expresses it) *at the right hand of God.*

This was the promise that He made when, for the last time, He drank wine with His disciples. "This is the *new covenant* in my blood". Translate this into words you can more easily understand:
"I will not leave you comfortless ... I seal this promise with my blood".

This is not God, betraying His own perfect character by *unjustly* punishing His own beloved Son for other people's crimes, but Jesus, working in perfect harmony with God — "The Father and I are *one*" — showing the fantastic depths of His love by sharing in all our pain and sorrow, in the hope that one day He can *win our love* and gather us into one family. He *volunteered* — God did not force Him and God *will never force us*.

Because we cannot see Him in the flesh, *we should never doubt* that in the *spirit* He is always available to us. But we must make the choice ourselves. He is there to help, to strengthen, to guide and to comfort, but not to coerce.

17

Balance

It cannot have escaped the notice of the reader that everything in life has its opposite. To mention just a few of the things with which we are familiar, there is dark and light, large and small, hot and cold, good and bad, bitter and sweet, love and hate, debit and credit and so on. Yet it is not quite accurate to use the term "opposite" in its usually accepted sense, for there are differing "degrees" of all these things, so that at times they can be relatively close to each other.

It is as if we might run along a scale in either direction from a given point, thus getting darker and lighter, better and worse, bigger or smaller and so on. In fact, there has to be a point of "balance" (rather like the point of balance on a set of weighing scales) if we are to be able to understand any of these ideas.

Now there is something important to notice about all this. It is something that we were taught in our earliest days at school, but with which we have become so familiar that we tend to forget the principle altogether. It is the fact that we cannot balance different values against each other.

You may say that a business man "weighs" the service he provides against the "cash" he receives, yet his ledgers will only reflect pounds and pence or dollars and cents. He balances "values". No amount of apples and pears can be said to equal so many sheep and goats, though a man may well be able to buy a sheep for so many apples or pears.

Perhaps you are wondering what all this has to do with religion or the life of the soul. The answer is simple. There are certain great *laws* of life which apply to everything in life, and when we try to fight against or ignore these *laws* we are heading for trouble. The *law* of "Balance" is one of them.

Let us take one particular point as an example. The state of "contentment" may be thought of as a balanced life. If your losses exceed your gains the balance is lost and you are unhappy. If someone does you an injury or a wrong, the balance is lost and you are unhappy. Instinctively you immediately attempt to restore the balance, and it is

here that so many people go astray because they do not pause long
enough to consider what values are involved.

Jesus gave us a very sound piece of advice which few people seem
prepared to take, yet which is of vital importance to every one of us.
He said: "Do not revenge yourself". Just look closely at this proposition. What are the values concerned when someone does you an
injury?

"In the old days", said Jesus, "men used to try to balance an injury
by putting another injury on the other side of the scales; an eye for an
eye, a tooth for a tooth".

The error lies in the fact that the values concerned are not eyes and
teeth but *right* and *wrong* — *good* and *evil*. The point of balance is
between good and evil, and when someone injures you, the scale has
tipped in the direction of evil. If you in turn injure your enemy, that
is also evil and cannot be put on the scale into the "pan" marked
"*good*". Thus the balance swings still more in the direction of evil.

The Apostle Paul put the matter very clearly when he said: "You
cannot overcome evil with evil, you can only overcome evil with good".
There is an old proverb which everyone knows and few honour, it is
this: "Two wrongs don't make a right — or two blacks don't make a
white".

At the beginning of this argument, it was said that if our losses
exceed our gains, the balance is lost — our contentment is gone. You
my be tempted to ask "What if our gains exceed our losses?" You
have a good point, for many people have made mistakes in this direction
too. They actually believe that their state of "well-being" will be
increased in proportion to their gains. But this is not true. The point
of balance is actually between our *needs* and our *supplies*, and though
we may labour under the delusion that our happiness will increase with
the increase of our supplies, it simply is not true. You may become
rich; you may become *powerful*, but the facts of history are all against
the idea that you are bound to become *happy*. The man who becomes
happy is the one who is wise enough to *give* as well as to *receive*.

Nor can you upset this idea by arguing that it is "out of balance"
to do good every day. Jesus told us, as has already been quoted, that
"sufficient for the day is the evil thereof". There is so much evil in this
world that it will take all our efforts each day in doing good, to restore
the balance.

You will see this principle of balance at work in every direction. You
have already seen how important it is not to eat too much or too little,

for this is the source of your energy and must be balanced against the body's output. And in the same way it is *necessary* for you to *work*. There is another old proverb which says that "all work and no play makes Jack a dull boy" — and it is true that relaxation is a vital necessity. But it is equally true that all pleasure and *no effort* is also a means of upsetting the balance, and cannot bring the happiness that some people fondly imagine.

This chapter would not be complete unless a reference were made to the necessity of also preserving a state of balance between what we might term "earthly" values and "spiritual" values, but this will be more fully dealt with in later chapters. Enough has been said at the moment to show how vital it is to preserve a perfect balance in all things. The intelligent person will surely grasp this point without difficulty, *but the most important lesson to learn* is not to mix your values — to attempt to rectify a deficiency in one direction by creating a surplus in another.

18

Freedom

Freedom is classed, in this twentieth century, as being one of the highest ideals of man. World statesmen regard it as almost the chief aim of organised society, and it is true that there is something in the soul of man that clamours for it. Yet there are very few other ideas about which there is so much confused thinking.

The very leaders whose aim it is to bring about freedom to mankind spend most of their time in drawing up codes, rules and regulations to ensure the inviolability of man's freedom, without a thought to the fact that all such codes are necessarily restrictive in their operation. It must surely be obvious that the freedom they have in mind must be purely relative.

Communists will seize and dominate a small country in order to force their own particular brand of freedom upon a reluctant people. There is a world-wide agitation for the "freeing" of the black races who are, in fact, not in any kind of physical bondage, and the youth of the world today is clamouring for freedom from the thoughts and ideas of the past.

Does Christianity have anything constructive to say upon this important issue? The organised "Church" has a great deal to say of course, but we have already seen very clearly that it is often — all too often — wide of the mark in its aims. We need to dig deeper, and to seek to discover the truth about *what Jesus had to say* on the matter.

First of all, it would be well to examine the conditions which prevailed during His lifetime, and the mental attitude of the people among whom He lived, for His first message was obviously directed to them and their particular situation.

His ministry was primarily amongst the Jews — the Hebrew people who must have been very concerned about this question of "freedom". They had had a long history of captivity. For many years they had actually been *slaves* — not merely a backward or underprivileged people, but mere chattels, *owned* by one of the most advanced and cultured races of the known world. Their owners or overlords were the Egyptians.

A few centuries later, after having established themselves as an independent and not unimportant nation, they were once more overwhelmed by a militarily superior power; uprooted from their homes and driven out of their cities to become slaves once more — this time in Babylon. Conditions were better than during that dreadful period in Egypt, but they were nevertheless again in captivity.

At long last, under Cyrus the Persian, they were once more given their freedom and became an independent nation. For about two hundred years they were more or less in control of their own destiny, but there followed another two hundred years under the domination, first of the Graeco-Egyptians and then the Graeco-Syrians. The Maccabean war led them again to independence, but this was short lived, lasting no more than eighty years before they were once more under domination — this time of the mighty Roman empire.

One may well imagine that thoughts of freedom filled the minds of the people to whom Jesus preached. The matter was more complicated than that, however. The poor people who, we are told, listened gladly to the Master, were not only in bondage to the Roman overlords, but also to their own religious leaders. They might have borne the domination of the foreigners as their fathers had borne that of the Babylonians, but the yoke of their religion lay heavier still upon their shoulders. They were a people almost without hope. The Pharisees, Sadducees and Scribes on the other hand, sought deliverance only from the Romans.

It follows, therefore, that Jesus was faced with a situation where the whole question of freedom must be dealt with. *Yet His only reference to freedom*, in the eighth chapter of St. John's Gospel, followed the incident when the Pharisees tried to trip Him up over the question of their law in the case of the woman taken in the act of adultery. It is very obvious that His statement had no reference whatever to politics. "If you continue to follow my advice you will know the *truth* —and the *truth* shall make you free".

Persistently His listeners tried to give His words a political meaning, but Jesus made it clear that there is a higher freedom, and stated plainly that the freedom He offered was the only real freedom. "Then shall ye be free indeed".

To a people whose greatest ambition was to shake off the shackles of a foreign power this declaration must have seemed strange indeed, and in all probability their minds flew back to the occasion when Jesus first addressed them in the synagogue in Nazareth. At that time, quoting a well known prophecy, He had said that God had chosen Him " . . . to proclaim release to the captives, and to set at liberty those who were bruised". Yet Jesus showed no inclination to oppose the Romans. His attitude had rather seemed to be one of appeasement. What did He mean then, by true freedom?

This leads us to look closely at our own experience. You already enjoy a state of political freedom, but are you really *free*? Is it not true that you are in bondage to all sorts of things? To mention one of the very least of your chains, you are in bondage to convention. There are all sorts of things that you cannot do without attracting undesirable attention to yourself. You cannot always wear even the kind of clothes you would like to wear because you are bound by the demands of fashion. Unwritten laws bind you as to how you shall prepare and eat a meal, how you shall behave in company, and how you shall conduct yourself in public. You are also bound by the rules and regulations of society which govern almost every aspect of your civilian existence, and by the laws of the land in which you live, and which control even your moral conduct.

These things are at times oppressive and wearisome, but there are even heavier chains which keep you in bonds. You are in bondage to your own fears; fears of the future; fear of failure; fear for your health; fear of pain and fear of death. But even that is not all. There is a bondage more difficult to shake off than all these. It is the tyranny of your own unconscious minds. The living computor which controls so much of your life, yet which you yourself cannot control. Little by little it has been fed down the years with all sorts of wrong data, so that it gives the wrong answer to all sorts of important questions, and leads you into courses of action which are not of your own *conscious* choosing, yet which you are powerless to check.

And just one part of this represents still another bondage — the bondage of "conscience" and guilt. Thus, when we speak of freedom, the term can only, at best, be relative. Nevertheless, knowing all these things, Jesus said that the *truth* shall make you "free indeed". There can surely be nothing more worth having than such a freedom. To be free of all the petty restrictions of life would be wonderful. To be free from fear and anxiety would be glorious, but to be free from the bondage of one's own conscience would be a liberty beyond words to describe. Is such a state really possible? You have the word of Jesus for it, and in all the centuries since He spoke those words He has never been proved to have lied.

To be able to make such a claim, Jesus must have experienced this freedom Himself, so first of all let us take a good look at His life. Four writers took the trouble to record all that could be remembered of Him, and though it is true that a great deal of each account was naturally repetitive (how could it have been otherwise) they would not have written if they had not felt that they also had something *new* to contribute. What was Jesus like as they remembered Him?

A few things stand out clearly. He was certainly free from *fear*. Surrounded by political enemies as He was, and in an age when a man could be summarily dealt with for even breathing a word of sedition, He openly declared His very revolutionary views in the presence of great crowds of people. On one occasion, in the very courts of the Temple, acting in a manner which would have ensured immediate seizure of any lesser person.

He was certainly free from *anxiety*, either about the present or about the future, and without hesitation gave up His work, His home, His friends and associations, and without money or even a change of raiment, set out upon His mission — a mission which would take several years to fulfil, and involve travelling from one end of the country to the other.

He was free from the bondage of *custom*, as was shown by the fact that, at a time when He needed above all things the goodwill of the people, He was for ever pulling down calumny upon His own head by breaking their customs and acting in a manner wholly foreign to their ideas of orthodoxy.

That He was free from the bondage of *conscience* is proved by the fact that every writer was utterly convinced above all things, that He was "without sin".

Did all this amount to anything? You have this unarguable testimony — that though He was a poor man, of undistinguished parentage, in an obscure little country forming a very tiny part of the mighty Roman Empire, and never achieved any notable deed beyond dying for His faith (and hundreds have done this) — His influence was such that every event in history is dated before or after His birth. No other single person has ever had so great an influence upon mankind, and about no other man have so many books been written. Yes, there is no doubt about it, Jesus is the living, *undying*, proof of His own claims, and He topped it all by saying: "*I am the truth*".

Now in a vague and unsatisfactory manner, Christians have accepted these facts for nearly two thousand years, but only as a sort of unattainable ideal, or as a theory believed in, but very rarely put to the test and proved. People have said: 'This I believe and accept", but it has been like accepting a cheque which is never deposited in the "bank" and is therefore never translated into hard cash. Such a cheque has, of course, never really been "accepted" in the true sense of the word.

Do you really believe in the possibility of the past being completely wiped out? Dare you put it to the test? Your unconscious mind tells you that you have sinned many times in the past. Your *new* belief or "faith" tells you that God has forgiven you. But have you accepted that forgiveness? Any skilled psychiatrist would prove to you after a few hours of investigation that you have not, and that is why, day after day, you continue to ask God for the forgiveness of sins which ought to have been blotted out of your memory after the first time of asking. There is a wonderful sense of release when you truly experience God's forgiveness, and a real feeling of having "been born again"

Are you utterly free from prejudice? You would be if the past were utterly wiped out. But the battle still goes on in your mind, and you cannot easily accept new ideas. You are hedged about by so-called Christian principles and precepts, many of which would be outraged by a complete "freedom". For too long you have thought of your conscience as "the voice of God within", and you dare not appear to defy it. Yet, as we have shown, it is in fact only the "voice of experience".

You know that Jesus said that "you must be born again", and you are prepared to accept the twentieth-century, watered down interpretation of this command. You are prepared to give up many wordly things, many so-called sinful things, and to make a "new beginning". But are you really prepared to give up *everything* you have ever held dear? Dare you start from the beginning as if you had *never known* anything else in your life?

Very few people have the courage to do quite this — and that is the reason why so few people have ever really found *the way*. Yet this is the price of true *freedom*. Jesus never said it would be easy. He warned His would-be followers that the whole world would probably condemn them. Freedom is *never* a gift. It always has to be bought with courage and sacrifice. Dare you reach out to take this wonderful thing? Remember that not only the world will suspect and condemn you — but your Church will probably be the first to cast a stone.

The first and hardest step is to accept the fact that God has truly blotted out *all* the past, and this is not achieved by merely "telling" yourself: "I believe" or "I am saved". John Wesley, of hallowed memory, once said: "Because I am *saved*, I know I cannot sin", yet within a year he was crying in despair: "Now I know that I am *not* saved — because I sin again and again".

Paul himself, who boasted of one thing only, that he had been *saved*, cried out "The things I would do, I do not, and the things I would not do, these I do . . . Oh wretched man that I am — who will *deliver me*?"

Neither of these men was really separated from God (the only true meaning of sin). The irregularities which caused them heartache were a "hang-over" from the past. They were measuring themselves, not against their love of God, but against standards that should have gone overboard when they met Jesus.

It is inevitable that certain habits of a lifetime cannot be overcome in a single instant. It is not impossible — for nothing is impossible with God — *but God also knows our human weakness, and never condemns the person who is making an honest effort.* Once you have realised this you will be well on the way to winning your battle, for the *worst* of your habits is that which tells you that *God is keeping a critical eye upon you* and frowning at your failures.

Now is the time to remember what the sacrifice of Jesus really means — to remember that He is available and *will be with you* all the time. Take Him everywhere — yes, even into *what you used to call sin.* This will be the acid test — not of His friendship, but of the genuineness of your conversion.

The next biggest help is to give yourself over to the task of *loving your fellow men;* good, bad, right and wrong; friendly or hostile; love them all. This does not mean "agree" with them; it does not mean lowering your standard to theirs; it does not even mean *liking* them; but love them enough to *pray for them;* to be concerned for them; to forgive them and to *serve* them. While you are doing this *you cannot be separated from God,* and therefore you cannot "sin".

This is the first real taste of freedom.

19

The Temple and the Church

Although, essentially, religion is a very personal matter, nevertheless, from the dawn of history, it has always been something which people have sought to share with each other.

Long before Christianity was thought of, buildings had been erected for the purpose of worship. Even where strange, uncivilised races have been discovered, it has been the common thing to find temples, altars and shrines dedicated to strange gods. And even when man has been utterly alone, there seems to have been some urge within him to build a temple or raise an altar immediately he has had a religious experience.

It is as though man, having come to a realisation that there is a God who created the world, and to whom he is therefore responsible in some vague sense, desires to build a special place — far superior to any "home" he may have enjoyed himself — where God may dwell.

Perhaps this is a pathetic effort to "tie God down" to a specific place where He may always be found. Perhaps it is an instinctive urge to do honour to the Great Creator. Perhaps it is even just another expression of the desire to propitiate or "keep on the right side" of the One who has power over life. Whatever may be the motive, the fact remains that the religious man, almost anywhere, seeks to have some form of "temple" in which to "worship" or perform his rites.

The Bible story of the origin and history of the Hebrew Temple is a fascinating and important one, but it is out of the scope of this present book. It is sufficient for our purpose to note the fact that Jesus accepted and conformed to the practice of His people with regard to worship in the Temple.

It is true that He warned the people not to put too great a trust in what was, after all, a "building made with hands". He emphasised the fact that the Temple itself was not imperishable, but He recognised the part it had to play in the lives of men and women.

In the early days of Christianity, after the disciples had had their

104

"Pentecostal" experience, they continued to worship in the Temple. The new truth taught to them by Jesus, quite obviously, did not involve them in such changes as leaving one Temple and building another.

It was, however, inevitable that, as more and more Gentiles were drawn into the new "Faith", a time would come when Christians would begin to build their own Temples. The important fact is that over the years these temples have come to be known by other names, and finally by a single name "Church".

This is unfortunate, because the word church really has nothing to do with buildings. The Greek word from which it originated means "called out", and even without the vital testimony of the New Testament, this alone would indicate that it refers to people and not to buildings. It is not quite clear at what stage the word Church was first used. In the Gospel story there is an occasion recorded where Jesus is supposed to have said "upon this rock I will build my Church", but most students of the Scriptures are agreed that this is most unlikely to have been a perfect interpretation of what Jesus actually said. It must be remembered that the Gospel was not written until almost forty years after the event, and by this time the word Church was in common use.

One thing is clear, however, and this is that the Church was regarded by the disciples as "the body of Christ" — His hands to do His work; His feet to run His errands; His voice to be used to continue His work and so on. The Temple, though we wrongly call it the Church, has come to have an important place in the life of Christian people, but the vital factor in Christianity is *and must remain*, the true *Church* — the Body of Christ, the people *called out* to do (or continue) the work of Jesus.

Where any group of people, having the redeeming work of Jesus at heart, meet together to discuss and further that work, or to prepare themselves for it, *the Church may be said to have met*. But it does not follow that where a group meet for the express purpose of "worshipping God", that the Church is in action.

Unlike many other religions, the early Christians sought to combine the two functions in one "service", People would meet for the purpose of worship — an act which involved certain rites and ceremonies according to their custom, but there would be added a period when the priest in charge, or one appointed by him would "preach" to the people or "teach" them and "exhort" them to follow the act of worship by a life of service to others. It seems very likely that the letters (epistles) of the disciples and Apostles were read to the people for this purpose, and this practice has continued down the ages.

Another practice of the early Church was for the people to share their experiences and to confess "to each other" their failures and faults. This was a reasonable thing in the days when the gathered company was rarely more than a handful of people, but obviously became more and more difficult as numbers grew. Today the practice has almost entirely disappeared and exists only among a few "peculiar" Sects. Where confession (of individuals) is practiced at all, it is always between the individual and the priest, and takes place in the utmost privacy. "Testimony" takes place only in certain evangelical groups and a few "Sects".

It seems certain that what is now known variously as The Sacrament of the Lord's Supper, Holy Communion or Mass, was an essential feature of every gathering of the Church, though not necessarily forming part of the Act of Worship, and probably not as a form of "Ritual". It had nothing to do with the priesthood, nor with any special place or temple. People who had accepted Jesus, and all that that involved, met in each other's homes as often as it was safe to do so, and without any elaborate ritual "shared this common meal together" — in remembrance of Him.

With the "Church" constituted as it is today, and especially in cases where several hundred members belong to one "congregation", it is difficult to see how the Lord's Supper could fail to undergo drastic changes in the way in which it was administered. But it is nevertheless a great loss to the Church that the original intimacy has vanished. It is safe to say that millions of people today partake of the Sacrament in much the same unthinking way as they repeat the Lord's Prayer. In fact, the Lord's Prayer has actually been woven into the fabric of the ritual which has made this Sacrament an integral part of the "worship" of the Church, without having any distinct bearing upon the "work" of the Church.

Jesus Himself dealt very largely with individuals and small groups of people, and though, at times, large numbers followed Him from place to place and listened to His "preaching", His ministry amongst the masses was never attended with any great success. Indeed, at the end, the only true "converts" remaining were those whom He had won as individuals.

This leads one to believe that the real work of the Church is unlikely to be effective if it is limited to the present system of gathering large congregations together into suitable buildings for weekly "services". This may be essentially the work of the Temple, but it leaves untouched the work of Jesus. While it undoubtedly has its value as an aid to spiritual development, it must not be confused with the real work to which every individual is "called" by the very nature of his conversion.

Essential though the "Temple" may be — and it will always have a place in any religion — let us remember that it is no more than "a place of worship", and it leaves much to be desired in the real growth of the soul. It is our opinion that in every congregation there should be smaller groups or "cells" whose purpose is not merely to worship or pay "homage" to our Maker, but to continue the work of Jesus, who expressed this idea with vivid clarity when He likened it to the work of the "yeast" in a mass of dough.

20

The Control of the Mind

It was said right at the beginning of this book that this is not a treatise. It is in fact a collection of thoughts, and of the discussions which arose from these thoughts, as a group of seeking people met regularly to experience a close communion with God, and to lay themselves open to the guidance of what has come to be known as "The Holy Spirit".

No attempt has been made to gather these thoughts into any special order, or to group them in any particular manner so as to form a sort of "formula" for living. It follows, therefore, that there is a certain "disorderliness" about the manner in which some of its subjects are grouped.

The reader may be tempted to think that this present chapter should have been a part of, or followed in sequence, the various chapters on the subject of *thought*. No apology is made. Each chapter, as it comes, should be treated on its merits. If it provokes constructive thought it will have achieved its purpose.

As we consider this complex organisation which we call a human being, we usually think of it in terms of "body", "mind" and "spirit". But there is something else — there is a sort of fourth dimension which we call the "soul".

It is often assumed that the words "spirit" and "soul" are merely different terms for the same thing, but this is not quite true. The word soul is derived from the Greek "psyche" and bears a relationship to the personality, whereas the word spirit comes from the Latin "spiritus" which means, literally, "breath" and is, in fact, what we might correctly call *the life force*.

Let is try to understand this complex unity of body, mind, soul and spirit. First of all there is the body. Everybody at least knows what we are talking about when we mention the body. It is a most complicated and fantastically efficient "machine" which is operated by what we might refer to as a "power house", or even more correctly, a vast "switch-board" which we call *the mind*.

It is obvious that there must be "something" which, to put it in terms that we can understand, *pulls the switches*. Now just as we can say that the mind controls the body, so we must infer that something also controls the mind. The important question is: what controls the mind?

There are, in fact, three things which can, in a sense, operate or control the mind. The first of these is what we might call (most truly) *the past*. A word of explanation is obviously necessary here, so that you can understand exactly all that is meant by "the past".

Incredible though it may seem, from the time that we are conceived — long before we are actually born — we have a special faculty which we have come to regard as, or call, a "memory". Everything that has ever happened to us is recorded in that memory. We might parallel this memory with the files of a great office — everything being duly sorted, docketed and filed in its proper place. As has already been said elsewhere in this book, we now have an even more apt comparison — that with a *computor*, a wonderful machine which in these days is being used more and more in almost any big business.

Everything that ever happens to us; the data concerning everything we see, everything we hear or feel; in fact everything we *experience*, is fed into this computor so that it may be readily accessible to guide us in any action which we may wish to make.

We should bear in mind, too, that when we first come into this world by the process of "birth", we come as "partly made" human beings. There is, of course, an incomplete body (no teeth etc.) but there is also a *mind*. It is an unconscious mind at this stage, only awakening to a conscious state when we are perhaps four, five or even six years of age. Until that stage, virtually all our actions are said to be Instinctive — that is to say, they are controlled by the unconscious mind.

In other words, the computor, which has all the data stored, gives the answer every time an action has to made; there is no thinking or "deciding" done. It is important to understand this, for we shall see how largely our minds are controlled by the past — in the sense that this computor contains only data which has been fed into it at some time in the "past".

Whenever we wish to do anything at all — to take any kind of action — it is as if we put a punched card into the computor — and asked a question. If we want to walk, we have to ask the question: "How can I walk?" The small baby, of course, has no answer to this question because it has had no experience — there is no data in the computor. So the child cannot yet walk. But, as the first few trials are made (with the help of some other person) data is gradually fed into the computor until it is able to give the right answers. It must be able to decide, for instance, where is the centre of gravity; what is the weight of the body, and many other things such as how to use the muscles; which muscles to use and what degree of energy to use. Once this data is in the computor the answer will come out very promptly and any action can be made without undue difficulty.

But the dangerous thing is that many other things are fed into this computor too. All the things, for instance, which the parents knew (or thought they knew), all the things that they feared, and the things that they believed and passed on to their children. The trouble is that we have an immense amount of data — not always accurate — built into our unconscious minds by the time we are born, and which will unconsciously shape our actions.

To give a small illustration, suppose you are sleeping in your bed, alone in your house. The room is dark. You know that there is no one else in the house, but suddenly you hear a noise as of someone moving in the room or taking a step. If this happens while we are conscious, having perhaps just awakened from our sleep, many things happen at once. First of all the computor within us tells us that there is something to be feared — if there was a noise, there must have been a person, and if such a person is there in the dark, then he can have no good intentions, and so various things begin to happen — completely unconsciously. For one thing — since the experience of the past tells us that there is likely to be a fight, so the adrenaline glands begin to work overtime. The heart begins to pump more vigorously in order to feed power to the various parts of our body which will be brought into action (that is why the heart begins to palpitate when we are afraid). Usually we experience a sensation which we hardly understand but which we call "the hair standing on end". As a matter of fact this goes right back to prehistoric days. In those days the human race was not quite as hairless as it is today. There was a good deal of hair on the back and chest and on the face and head. Like many other animals, the creature, when attacked, would try to make itself as fearsome as possible in the hope of frightening off the aggressor. In fact, in those days, the hair really did stand on end. It can no longer do so in quite the same way. Modern methods of hairdressing and facial shaving make this impossible, and there is usually very little hair on a person's back, but nevertheless the human computor sends out its ancient signal — we go through the motions, as it were — and still, to this day, have the feeling that the hair is indeed standing on end. These things are mentioned only to show what a powerful hold the past still has over our actions. We think we are doing *only what we want to do*, but in fact, we are doing what the *past* tells us to do.

This is particularly noticeable in the realm of what we call religion, but is usually little more than superstition. Interestingly enough the dictionary definition of "superstition" is *"false religion"*. We believe certain things about God, about the "next world", about all sorts of "spiritual" things, *not because we have had any experience of them*, but because our parents, our grandparents and our great-grandparents have believed them and have instilled them into the minds of their children. So it is that we have preconceived ideas about ourselves and about our relationship with what we call God. Most of these ideas are wrong. Most of them are not in fact true religion at all, but *superstition*.

The second thing which controls our mind is our environment. As small children, as growing children and as adolescents we come under the influence of parents, teachers, friends, and all the people among whom we live and work from day to day. We also come under the influence of *things* as well as people, and so there is a second power at work to complicate the delicate business of controlling our own minds, making our own decisions and deciding upon our own actions .All too often the decisions we make are our unconscious response to these "outside" pressures. We *think* that we have "made up our own minds" when in fact our decision is the result of the pressure of our environment.

The third, and by far the most important thing that controls the mind is what might be called *our real self*. This "thing" has a name. In Greek it is "the Psyche" which, truly interpreted is the *soul*.

Very often, and quite wrongly, we use the term "spirit" which comes from the Latin "spiritus" and means "the life force". Now the life force, if we trace it back far enough, is *God Himself* — it is certainly part of that life force that activates us or makes us "alive". But this is not the soul. The "life force" operates through the body and the mind for a certain number of years: until, in fact, they are either "worn out" with age, damaged irreparably by disease, or destroyed by some accident. But there is no evidence that any of these things destroys the soul. Indeed there appears to be a whole mass of evidence quite to the contrary.

We need to be very careful in distinguishing between the "spirit" and the "soul". There is a Greek word used frequently in the New Testament — unhappily often translated as "ghost", but sometimes as "spirit" — it is the word "pneuma" from which we have derived such words as "pneumonia" and "pneumatic" (having to do with *breathing* or *air pressure*. The word had its origin in the fact that it had been observed from time immemorial that when a creature ceased to breathe it ceased to live; it was dead. *Pneuma* (breath), therefore came to be considered as the "life force".

In religion this word was frequently thought of as referring to "the breath of God", and it was believed that God had "breathed" into all living creatures. The "Hagion Pneuma" (Holy Spirit), literally means *the spirit "set apart"*, and has no other meaning than *God — active*. It would therefore help us in our thinking to reserve this word Spirit for the Spirit of God, or any "part" of that Spirit operative in "living" creatures — in other words, *"life"*. For all other purposes we should use the word *psyche* (*the real self*). Perhaps we should understand this term better if we thought of it as the *personality*. It is that part of any human being which differs from any other even when every other part seems to be the same.

There is one small point which might be introduced here, though it is not our intention to discuss it at length. If, as many people believe, there is a possibility of contact between living people and people who have already "died" as far as the world is concerned, then thet contact will be a contact with the "soul" of the departed, and not the "spirit", as is generally believed. We may discuss this point at greater length later in this volume.

To get back to the subject of "the control of the mind", it ought to be obvious from what has been said, that if we wish to experience a "full" and satisfying life, we must somehow discard to a very large extent, the influence of the *past*, and control the influence of *environment*. We should, in fact, make sure that it is our psyche which is *in charge*. This means that we refuse to be merely "victims" of circumstance or of other people's thinking and planning. The *perfect* state is obviously that in which our *psyche* is "tuned-in" to the Great Spirit — to God Himself. And surely this is exactly what Jesus meant when He suggested that the only way in which we could experience the "life more abundant" was to begin by "repenting", (a word which means *"changing our minds"*). In other words, discarding the outworn thinking of a bygone age, and accepting the *new ideas* which He was bringing.

This is not an easy matter. Jesus Himself never suggested that it would be. In fact He pointed out very clearly that "the way is narrow, and few there be that find it". And when He used the word "narrow", He did not mean it to suggest that we must be "narrow-minded". There were few people with whom He could not get on well, and the ones He disliked most of all were the people whom we, today, would classify as being narrow minded — people in fact with "closed" minds that refused to accept any new idea.

The best way in which to set about the difficult task of controlling our own minds and coming into perfect harmony with God, is to increase the amount of time that we give to silence and meditation. It is in these periods that we can come closest to God. The oftener that we sit in silence with Him, the more will our power grow. We must abolish superstition from our minds — and this will probably mean getting rid of all our preconceived ideas of religion — and accept the basic fact that God made us for Himself and desires to *use us* for His purposes. He does not *need* us to talk to Him, but He does need *us to listen to Him*. We must have faith to believe that as we come into harmony with God we will have such control of our minds (and this means the mighty potential that is within us) that there can be no such thing as sickness or evil within us because every part of the body, every cell in the body, every movement will be controlled by *us*. Not by the past; not be our enviromnent; not by a mental computor which has been programmed by other people, but by the Psyche (unlimited in power because it is in harmony with the Divine Source of *all power*).

The only limits to our power are the limits which we have either set ourselves, or allowed others to set for us. Once we have accepted the idea that God's limitless Power can work through us, and are prepared to give it full reign, there are no limits at all. "The works that I have worked — and greater works than these — shall ye work also *if ye believe*" said Jesus.

Our first aim, therefore, is to come into "tune" with the Infinite for by this means we become free from the ties that have bound us for most of our lives. "The *truth* shall set you *free*" said Jesus. But the purpose behind it all is not purely selfish. If it were, then we would have little hope of ever achieving the harmony we seek. We must certainly learn to have complete control of our own minds, but having got so far, our next objective is to use the power thus liberated to help others.

In order to do this, it may become necessary for us, for a time at least, to learn to control the minds of others. When Jesus said to a lame man: "Take up thy bed and walk," He was doing precisely this. The whole process of healing others "spiritually" is based upon this. The "laying on of hands" is a part of the process. It is necessary to make physical contact with the patient in order that the "power" that has been liberated within ourselves is passed on to him or her.

But when we attempt to "heal" others, it is vitally necessary that all the old influences which once controlled our minds should have been washed away. The psyche, fully attuned to God, must be in charge. Such negative thoughts (belonging to the past) as "suppose we don't succeed" or "suppose the sick person does *not* get well" or again "suppose the patient does not have sufficient faith" must be completely absent. As James the brother of Jesus put it: "let not that man think that he can achieve anything".

As we place our hands upon the sick person we must allow the psyche to take charge completely. Our minds must be so controlled that we can see only a *healed* body before us — only a *happy* person, a *relieved* person — and thus we pass on to this person the *certainty* of being healed. This is the secret of what has so often been inaccurately called "spiritual" healing, but which is more correctly "psychological" healing, because it is healing through the operation of the psyche. This is the first and most important lesson we must learn if we would prepare ourselves for healing work. And let us remember that the call of Jesus was not only to "preach the Gospel" to all creatures, *but "to heal the sick"*.

21

The Meaning of Repentance

When John the Baptist came preaching to the people of Galilee and Judaea, he claimed that his purpose was to fulfil the ancient prophecy to "Make straight a path for the Lord" — to prepare the way for the Messiah. And the burden of his message was a call to *repent*.

It is a sad fact that whatever the people of that generation may have understood by his message, the people of more modern days have been completely in error as to his true meaning.

The word "repentance" has come to be associated with "remorse". We use the word as if it meant that we were being called upon to be "sorry for" or to "regret" certain things. In fact it means nothing of the kind. The Greek word *"metanoia"* which has been translated in the New Testament as "repentance" means literally "to have another mind" or, to put it simply, "to change our mind".

In the light of what was written in the last chapter of these notes, we see how important this distinction is. The Jewish people had for centuries been led to believe that unless they followed exactly the long and difficult code of *laws* which began with the "Ten Commandments" and for a thousand years had been added to and elaborated by the "tradition of the Elders", they were doomed to destruction. This left the vast majority of the people without hope, for there was nothing in their religious code that made provision for turning a "bad" man into a "good" one.

It is worthy of note, in passing, to mention that even in the Hebrew tongue, in the Old Testament, the word translated as "repentance" was the Hebrew *"nocham"* which strictly interpreted means *"comfort"*. This obviously also has nothing to do with remorse or sorrow.

Let us pause for a moment to consider what life is all about. We are born into this world without being consulted in the matter. We are not asked if we would like to come — we have no option. All history and tradition tells us that we shall have a limited time here, which, barring accidents, may be a matter of seventy or eighty years. For the first twenty of these years, or a little less, we shall be under certain restraints, and far from free to do as we wish. And for the last ten years we may well be so weak and worn out that we have neither the desire nor the strength to contend with life's difficulties. Thus we are perhaps, heirs to about fifty years which we might call our own. What is the highest aim and purpose of these years?

Of course it is quite true that a great number of people never give even a thought to the matter. They suffer what they must, with or without complaint according to their particular bents. They snatch whatever relief or advantage comes their way, without much concern for its effect upon anybody else or any other sphere of life, and they face death as something perhaps a little frightening, but nevertheless inevitable. Sometimes they are fatalistic enough to brush the whole experience of life aside with the remark that "what is to be will be".

There are many who cannot or will not face realities, and who seek relief in any kind of pleasure, hating every moment when circumstances force them to do the things that bring no obvious pleasure. Sport, cinemas, theatres, television, drink, food, talk and reading are to them varying types of escapism.

There are a few, born perhaps with rebellion in their hearts, who seek to dominate life and to turn everything to their own use and advantage — power seekers who cannot bear any kind of opposition.

Others again feel that health of body is the chief objective of life. "Give me my health and strength", they say, "and I will ask for nothing more". It may well be that a deeply hidden unconscious fear of pain gives rise to this attitude.

And, of course, there are those who are born with a violent acquisitive instinct, who are concerned largely with the making of money and acquiring of all and every kind of property.

Yet when we examine closely all these varied types, is it not true that, in fact, they are all seeking the same thing — happiness? The money maker believes that he can "buy" happiness. The health seeker believes that happiness lies in good health. The power seeker can only be "happy" when not opposed, and the pleasure seeker can only find happiness in refusing to face facts.

It seems perfectly clear, and it is certainly very logical, that the great aim of life is to find *peace and happiness* — a state which may otherwise be described as one of perfect *harmony*. The great tragedy is that religion, having found no method, and no hope, of achieving this state on earth, has compromised by regarding it as a *reward* in the life to come for having reached certain standards of "perfection" in this life.

The most shocking feature of Christianity is the fact that, in the last hundred years at least, evangelistic preachers have grasped at straws and claimed that the reward may be very simply won by "calling upon the Name of Jesus", and that by His death all errors that have militated against the perfect state have been magically washed out. This is making a mockery of the whole purpose of the life and teaching of Jesus.

In St. John's Gospel, chapter ten and verse ten, Jesus clearly defines His purpose with regard to humanity. "I am come", He says, "that they might have life, *and that they might have it more abundantly*".

There is absolutely nothing here to suggest for one moment that Jesus is referring to any other life than the life lived here upon the earth. His words conjure up the thought of a life more satisfying, more complete, than anything we have yet known.

There is nothing very satisfying in the life that is lived by the great majority of people in any given age. Certainly there was nothing in the lives of the people to whom Jesus was speaking at that time. In fact their lives were hedged about with petty rules and regulations which governed and restricted their every movement. The domination of the Romans who were in charge of their country was not nearly so oppressive as some people imagine, for there, as in so many other countries, the Romans brought law and order and material progress. The real yoke on the necks of the people was the intolerable business of trying to live up to the demands of their own religion. They were confined in a "straight-jacket", of rules and regulations, and in bondage to a conscience which was the direct result of hundreds of years of wrong religious teaching. The only possibility of "salvation" for these people lay in throwing off this yoke — *in changing their minds*, (minds that had been warped by the traditions of the past).

No amount of regret or remorse for all the petty breaches of the *law* could ever have set them free, nor given them a fuller life, for they would still have been faced with the long future of striving to achieve the impossible.

Paul takes us a step further even than this. He claimed that as far as the Law was concerned, he was in fact perfect. He was one of the few who had actually been able to observe and obey every detail of the Law, *yet still had not found happiness* — that sense of fulfilment for which had had been seeking, *until he found the way of Jesus*. This

118   *Out of the Silence*

is most important because it confirms once more that a *complete change of mind* is necessary before we can find the fullness of life which Jesus sought to bring us.

For too long people have been taught that what they call "conscience" is the voice of God speaking to them. In fact it is nothing of the kind. It is the voice of "tradition", or, if you like, "habit". *It is the voice of the past* which, if we do not check it, will take charge of our minds and destroy any hope we may have of peace and happiness.

Reading in the Acts of the Apostles, we find that on every occasion when people accepted the Gospel of Jesus, "they went their way rejoicing". This, in spite of the fact that the very acceptance of Jesus placed them in jeopardy. We cannot escape the fact that the early Church was a group of *happy* people.

All their religious leaders, all their wise men and all their experts told them that it was *wrong* to believe in this new doctrine, and threatened them with dire penalties if they continued to do so, but it made no difference.

Going further afield than the Holy Land, we find that people everywhere who heard and accepted the Gospel were always affected in the same way, even in defiance of the mighty Roman Empire which had all the power in the world to force its own ideas upon the people.

Now let us turn our thoughts to the Christian Church of our own day. Would it be true to say that it is remarkable for the "happiness" of its people? Is the sense of rejoicing so obvious that people outside the Church cast envious glances at it? We know, if we face the facts honestly, that the reverse is the case. It is a rare thing indeed when a stranger, coming into contact with Christian people, says: "Ah! this is what I have been searching for". Indeed, the sad truth is that the Church is so lacking in any kind of appeal or vitality, that it does not even arouse opposition.

But let us look at the matter from another angle. Is there not a distinct similarity between the Church of today and the religious atmosphere into which Jesus stepped with His revolutionary ideas? Is it not true that our Church leaders stand where the Scribes and the Pharisees stood — urging upon the people a newer, but no less onerous code of rules and regulations, which are just as heavy a burden as "the tradition of the elders?" Is it not true that the voice of "conscience" is even more pointedly regarded as the voice of God?

There is one important distinction of course, and that is that Christianity does give a hope to the hopeless. It *does* claim to be able to take a "bad" man and give him a chance to become a "good" man. But let us see what happend to such a man. On "conversion" he rejoices in the knowledge that his "sins" are forgiven, and that he is given another chance — a new start in life. But *the voice of his conscience is not stilled.* In fact it becomes increasingly lively. In the shortest possible time, the "joy of salvation" is squeezed out of him and he finds himself fighting an endless battle against the terrible odds of daily temptation.

Paul himself experienced this very thing and cried out: "Oh wretched man that I am . . . the very things I would not do, these I do, and the things I know I ought to do, I do not. Who can save me?" (Romans 7, verses 15, 19, 24.)

John Wesley, in more recent times, reached a similar point in his experience when he said: "I know that because I am *saved* I cannot sin — yet every day I sin and do the very things I would not do. Therefore I can only believe that in fact I am not yet saved".

It is never a good thing to quote single verses of Scripture to prove a single particular point. Such verses must always be seen in their complete context, and for this reason you are recommended to read particularly the whole of the seventh chapter of Paul's letter to the Romans, and to pay special attention to the first six verses. Paul is saying here, as clearly as possible, exactly what is pointed out in this present chapter of these notes.

Jesus said that "The *truth* shall make you free". Free from what? Certainly not the bondage of Rome. Certainly not from all the obligations of any social structure. Surely not from the leadership of their own religion.

The one thing above all others from which we must be set free is the bondage of the past; the wrong ideas; the prejudices; the incorrect data that has been fed into the computors of our minds for generations. In other words *we must change our minds* — we must *repent.*

Let us quote a few small illustrations to make this point abundantly clear.

A small boy stepped carelessly off the pavement one day, right into the path of an approaching lorry. The driver slammed on his brakes but was quite unable to avoid hitting the child, yet stopped so suddenly that the front wheels of his vehicle were actually resting on the body of the unfortunate victim. A man who witnessed the accident and saw the position of the body sprang forward impulsively and grasped the front bumper of the lorry and lifted the vehicle free so that others could pull away the child.

A passing news reporter was the only person to realise that the man had performed an extraordinary feat, and made enquiries to find out if the man was a potential world record breaker in the field of weight lifting. Imagine his amazement when tests proved that the man in question was quite incapable, under any ordinary circumstances, of lifting even a quarter of the weight that he had lifted when freeing the child. Under great emotional stress his "conditioned" mind had temporarily forgotten the self imposed limits of his own strength. Normally his mental "computor" would have told him that he could not lift more than one hundred and twenty pounds. But in the present instance he had been concerned with only one thing — to lift a lorry (regardless of its weight) from the body of a child. In this emergency his real self (his soul) had been moved by compassion and had ordered his muscles to do a certain job and he had done it — lifting a matter of eight hundred pounds with considerable ease.

In a test carried out at a certain university in America, a young girl, under hypnotic influence, was ordered to leave the room and go into an adjoining field to count the heads of cotton. She was to return in exactly three minutes. Any so-called "sane" person would have declared this task to be utterly impossible. She returned exactly on time and gave the number of heads — later carefully checked and found to be quite correct. The number was so high that any average person, without leaving the room, could not have counted mentally in so short a time. The value of the experiment lay in proving that our efficiency is only limited by our convictions. The mind tells us that we cannot do a thing, but when a personality (soul) takes over (and this is what happens under hypnosis) there are virtually no limits.

Jesus said: "If ye shall say to this mountain: 'be ye cast into the middle of the sea' *and believe it*, it will happen". He never doubted His own power, and He told His disciples very clearly that they would be able to work even greater works than His own. There was only one condition: they must first repent (change their minds) — get rid of all the accretions of bygone ages of error, and *believe* that as they came into perfect harmony with God, no good thing would ever be impossible.

All this is very interesting, but there will naturally be those who immediately see the dark side of the picture. They will probably suggest that all this would lead a person to believe that there can be no such thing as sin: that, indeed, being free from conscience, we can do as we like.

Paul, of course, saw this very point and tried to argue his case in the above quoted chapter of Romans. In reading his many letters it becomes obvious that many members of the early Church actually fell into this trap, but Jesus, who also saw the point quite clearly said: "Think not that I am come to destroy the *law* or the prophets. I am come *not to destroy but to fulfil*". (Mat. 5:17)

What exactly did Jesus mean by saying on the one hand that He had not come to destroy the Law, and on the other hand by suggesting that there is an escape from its bondage? There can be no better way of answering this question than by taking a close look at the life and example of Jesus.

To be able ever to understand Jesus, it is necessary to know more than a little of the true background of Jewish history, and the best place to find our knowledge is in the Old Testament.

Let us admit at once that a great part of this wonderful Book is very difficult to understand. Some portions add little or nothing to our knowledge as far as it relates to the teaching of Jesus, and some is of value only to historians and theologians. But through it all, as has already been remarked, there runs like a golden thread, a theme which finds its true interpretation only in Jesus.

The early part of the Book of Genesis, in which probably at least five writers had a part, gives us an ideal starting place. For too long this was regarded as a factual record of the process of creation and the birth of mankind, with the result that constant friction has occurred between religious and scientific bodies. Even in this enlightened age in which we live, there are millions of people who refuse to accept the idea of evolution on no better grounds than that it conflicts with the Genesis story.

The future may well prove that our present ideas of evolution are as erroneous as were our ideas that the world was once part of the sun, but it will not be the book of Genesis which corrects us because this unique record was never written nor intended as a scientific treatise.

On the contrary, the writers appear to have attempted to set out, almost in children's story book form, a theory which explains the relationship between God and man, and this is the basis of all religion.

For the purpose of religious understanding it is unimportant by what means God created man. It is sufficient to realise that He established between Himself and this highly intelligent creature a unique relationship. One of the Genesis writers pictures God as walking in the garden and speaking in intimate terms with man. In other words, he is telling us that there was a point in human history when indeed a close and perfect understanding existed between God and man.

It is significant that, according to Genesis, this ideal state collapsed when man "ate of the tree of knowledge of good and evil". Can this possibly be anything other than a symbolic method of explaining the very point dealt with in the earlier part of this chapter? At this point Adam and Eve became conscious for the first time that they were naked. Is this not the beginning of the thing we call "conscience"? A man in perfect harmony with God can do no wrong. It is when a man attempts to do things without taking God into account that he begins to run off the rails.

In this picture story of Genesis, man is shown as doing furtively the very thing that God had warned him against, and as a result he was cast out of the garden. In plainer language, he was for the first time *out of harmony* with God and thus *had put himself out of the* garden.

Variations on this theme are played throughout the early chapters, and by the time of Moses, there was such mental conflict in the minds of the people that some "official" simplification became necessary. So the *law* (the Ten Commandments) came into being. This laid down a moral and social code sufficiently sound to have been adopted as the basis of Law in almost every civilised country in the world.

The sad fact, however, is that by this time there was so little communion with God, and so few people in harmony with Him, that to deal with the matter the religionists found it necessary to enlarge the code until it was not *ten* but many hundreds of Commandments. And all the while the thing called conscience grew and grew.

By this time, in the Bible story, the world is pictured as a busy place. Stories give place to histories, and we see in the crowded towns and cities very few people who "hear the voice of God" any more. Only the prophets — almost always dwellers in the wilderness or mountainous places — take time out to "be still and know God".

The situation becomes more and more hopeless, and the real thinkers of religion begin to realise that a violent upheaval in religious thinking among the masses will be necessary if man is ever to escape from the web he has spun for himself. The general belief is that God Himself will take drastic action, and prophecies of a Messiah begin to appear and to become more and more frequent.

This, virtually, is the story of the Old Testament. There is no time here to analyse the whole Book more minutely, but this is undoubtedly the theme, and it is into this atmosphere aggravated by several hundred more years of human experience, that Jesus finally came — "in the fullness of time".

John paved the way by telling the people that the time had come for them to *change their minds* (repent). From here we can go on to examine the life and teaching of Jesus.

22

The Life and Teaching of Jesus Christ

Let us look, first of all, dispassionately, at the life and character of Jesus. This is not as easy as it seems because most people have preconceived ideas — the result of teaching received in their infancy, backed up by sentimental hymns and a good deal of art which, in the main, expresses the feelings of the artists rather than describing the Man.

We could say in all truth that there is no reliable picture available, and little authentic information. Therefore, in one sense, nobody can tell us just what Jesus was like. Historians and theologians alike, in seeking the truth about Jesus, have fallen into the trap of trying to make Him conform to certain ideas which nearly two thousand years of Christianity have built up.

After nearly four hundred pages of his book *In quest of the Historical Jesus*, Albert Schweitzer sums up by saying: "The Jesus of Nazareth who came forward publicly as the Messiah, who preached the ethic of The Kingdom of God who founded the Kingdom of Heaven upon earth and died to give His work its final consecration *never had any existence*".

This is a Doctor of Divinity and Doctor of Philosophy speaking, after years of intense study, *but he did not mean that Jesus never existed* — he meant that the Jesus built up in the minds of theologians, writers and preachers over two thousand years, is more myth than reality.

Silvester Horn gives a more realistic picture, based on what we know and can observe. This is what he wrote: "Conceive a strong and strenuous Jewish workman, alive to all the delights of nature, and with the crowning joy of a pure heart and a clear conscience, and an invigorating consciousness of God; conceive a massive head and a rugged face marked with thought and sympathy, but with the mystic light of moral victory always there; conceive dark flashing eyes, that can speak easily inspiration or indignation, and you have the figure that wanders

124

through my dreams, the Happy Warrior behind whom I hope to fight till I die".

How oddly this contrasts with such sickly sentimental words as are contained in a popular hymn.

Gentle Jesus, meek and mild, look upon a little child,

Pity my simplicity, suffer me to come to Thee.

It was no meek and mild Jesus who ruthlessly drove the money changers out of the courts of the Temple and overturned their tables. It was no meek and mild pious poseur who denounced the powerful Scribes and Pharisees and called them "play actors" (hypocrites).

The Romans, who were renowned for their courage, regarded the Jews as a race of snivelling cowards, but when Jesus stood before Pilate, that important official was so impressed that an exclamation broke from his lips "Ecce, homo!" (Behold a *man!*)

There seems little doubt that Jesus began life as a carpenter, but it is equally clear that He "rose from the ranks" to become a teacher, holding the title of Rabbi, which argued that he must have taken the Rabbinic Course, and was entitled to teach within the Synagogue.

We know little of His early life, but there seems to be no doubt that He, at one time, lived with the sect of the Essenes—a group of monk-like students of life and religion cut off from all civilian life, and living in caves in the mountainous regions. The Nazarenes were one such group and Jesus was known as "the Nazarene", not because He came from Nazareth, but because He belonged to that ancient religious sect. Sampson, hundreds of years before the town of Nazareth was built or thought of, was also a Nazarite.

We know that Jesus was an ardent student of the Scriptures, and there seems to be no doubt that He read and understood the deep truths lying behind the myths and superstitions, and recognised Himself as the One who should come. One might express it as "feeling the call of Messiahship".

There can also be little doubt that Jesus was indeed a rugged and healthy young man. There is evidence that during the three years of His ministry, He travelled four times from Galilee to Jerusalem and three times returned — and all this was done on foot. A total of over a thousand miles on difficult and dangerous roads.

He was utterly unconventional, constantly arousing the enmity of the upper classes by His refusal to comply with the social and religious customs of His day. He was the social and educational equal of the Pharisees, as is shown by the fact that He was more than once invited into their homes to eat a meal. Yet He chose His friends from such people as James and John (the sons of thunder), the revolutionary Judas, and the "fifth columnist" Matthew.

Everything about this young man breathes of *health and freedom* and sheer confidence in His own ability (backed by a God with whom He walked in the closest communion). He made many powerful enemies because He would not compromise with them, yet never showed the slightest sign of *fear*. Here was a man who *lived* the things He taught, and proved by His own life that the message that He preached to the people was no mere theory, but solid, unshakeable *truth*.

He taught that the "truth should make us *free*". Jesus Himself was free; free from the bondage of the past (conscience, convention and custom); free from *anxiety* (He took no thought for tomorrow, knowing that His God would provide); free from *fear* (He did what He must and went where the Spirit led in spite of all opposition); He was free from *sickness*, though He would touch a leper and walk among the throngs of sick and diseased people whose healing formed so great a part of His ministry; He was free from *sin* for He was never separated from His God.

He taught that men should *deny* themselves and live for others, and every bit of evidence shows that Jesus lived up to this standard. Neither His worst enemy nor His best friend would have called Him "pious", but none would doubt the deep compassion that burned in His heart for all who suffered, nor the fact that He translated His sympathy into practical help. The truest thing ever said about Jesus was that "He went about *doing* good" (not *being* good).

Jesus taught that once a man had found the truth, he must allow *nothing* to shake his conviction, not even the influence of his closest friends or relations. But more than this; he must show his convictions *openly* and not in secret. In that age a man was often sentenced to death for relatively superficial offences, and death was by crucifixion. A condemned man was compelled to carry his own cross to the place of execution, and the nature of his crime was printed on a placard nailed to the top of the cross. Jesus seemed to have this in mind when He said that "if a man will follow me, he must take up his cross".

In His last recorded talk with His disciples, Jesus said that there was only one way by which a man would be recognised as one of His followers: "that you love one another, even as I have loved you".

One more very important aspect of the character and life of Jesus

must be noted. *He was a positive thinker.* He believed that all things
were possible to those who walked in harmony with God. *And He
believed this, not only of Himself.* Clearly He told His listeners that they
could do even greater works than He Himself had performed if they
fulfilled the one great condition of *believing.* Jesus was two thousand
years ahead of His time when He made this pronouncement, but in
our last chapter we showed how science is able to prove the truth of
what Jesus taught.

It was James, the brother of Jesus, who pointed out to the people to
whom he was writing how necessary it was to have a rock-like faith:
"But let him ask in faith, nothing wavering. For he that wavereth is
like a wave driven of the wind and tossed. Let not that man think that
he shall receive anything".

Outside the Bible and the somewhat doubtful record of stories told
by followers of Jesus (many of which cannot be fully authenticated)
there is little information to be found about Jesus, but what there is
fully confirms the above assessment of His character.

In the year 62 A.D. (this figure has been corrected to our modern
calendar) a Roman physician named Aesculapius Cultellus wrote to
his nephew serving with the army in Syria. He had apparently been
called upon to treat a sick man named Paul — a Roman citizen of
Jewish parentage who, from the description given was undoubtedly
Paul the Apostle. From Paul he learned something about Jesus and
therefore asked his nephew to make enquiries while in Jerusalem. The
nephew was one Gladius Ensa, a captain of the VII Gallic Infantry,
who replied some six weeks later. Below are a few extracts from his
letter.

"I asked . . . if he had ever heard of the famous Messiah who was
killed while still a young man. He said that he remembered it very
clearly because his father had taken him to Golgotha (a hill just outside
the city) to see the execution . . . He gave me the address of one Joseph
who had been a personal friend of the Messiah . . . This morning I
went to call on Joseph. His memory was clear and from him I got an
account of that happened. In the year 783, Pontius Pilatus (Governor
of Judaea and Samaria) was called to Jerusalem on account of a riot. A
certain young man (the son of a carpenter in Nazareth) was said to be
planning a revolution against the Roman Government. Strangely
enough our own intelligence officers who are usually well informed
appear to have heard nothing about it, and when they investigated the
matter, they reported that the carpenter *was an excellent citizen* and

that there was no reason to proceed against him. But the old-fashioned leaders of the Jewish faith, according to Joseph, were much upset. They greatly disliked his popularity with the poorer Hebrews. They told Pilatus that the "Nazarene" had publicly claimed that a Greek or a Roman or even a Philistine, who tried to live a decent and honourable life was quite as good as a Jew. Pilatus was not impressed with this argument, but when the crowds threatened to lynch Jesus, he decided to take him into custody to save his life . . . Pilatus talked to Jesus for several hours and asked him about the "dangerous doctrines" which he had preached. But Jesus answered that he never referred to politics. He was not so much interested in the bodies of men as in man's soul. He wanted all people to regard their neighbours as their own brothers and to love one single God, who was the Father of all living beings".

The letter goes on to tell how Pilate finally, to save his own reputation, sacrificed his prisoner who was crucified amidst the howls and laughter of the Jerusalem mob. He concludes: "That is what Joseph told me, with tears running down his old cheeks. I gave him a gold piece when I left him, but he refused it and asked me to hand it to one poorer than himself".

Jesus said on one occasion (John 10:10) "I am come that they might have life, and that they might have it more abundantly". From what we know of His character, He Himself lived a full and abundant life.

23

But what is God?

It has been said before in these notes that true religion deals only with the relationship between God and man. It has also been said many times that the degree of happiness, or the sense of fulfilment in life, is directly proportionate with the degree of *harmony* between a person and God.

We have followed closely the teaching of Jesus and other great teachers on the subject of life and its meaning and purpose, and its vast potentialities, and we always come up against the same tremendous problem — this relationship between man and God.

By this time we should have a fairly clear idea of what man is, but we may well doubt whether the average person has any sort of clear idea of what God is. It is perhaps significant that the Icelandic word *godi* means "the unknown", though we do not suggest that this was the origin of the word God.

The average person is not a theologian, and even if he could be persuaded to read the best books by the acknowledged authorities on the subject, it is doubtful whether he would be very much wiser. It is even doubtful whether the theologians have any *real knowledge* to impart.

Nor is it very helpful to refer people to the Bible as the one great source of knowledge. For one thing, thousands of years of study by every kind of expert have not produced any sort of uniformity of belief in what God is.

We have already dealt with one aspect of this matter in our third chapter, but that was intended essentially for those people who have already accepted the *fact* of God.

Let us go deeper now. The writer has had a great deal of experience in dealing with High School children — "teenagers" — who, in the light of modern science, have begun to have doubts about the reality of the things they were taught in Sunday School, and at times even about the reality of God. "If there is a God, what is He like?"

To get any clarity at all, we must, of course, start at the beginning, and this would seem to lie in the question "Is there, in fact, such a thing or person as God at all?"

However long the Universe has been in existence, common sense tells us that there must have been a time when it was not. There must have been a beginning. The question then arises: "Did it happen by design or by accident?" At least one well known scientist has dared to suggest that the whole universe is nothing but a vast "accidental collocation of atoms".

It is almost incredible that any intelligent person could ever have reached such a conclusion. One might as well suggest that a few thousand cut-out letters thrown up into the air could fall to earth in the form of one of Shakespeare's immortal plays. Let us quote a simple little illustration.

The seeds of the Namaqualand Daisy and the seeds of the common parsnip are so alike in appearance that it would be almost impossible to distinguish the one from the other. Furthermore, if a quantity of each were reduced to fine powder and submitted to an expert chemist for analysis, they would be found to be identical. Now the amazing thing is that when these seeds are planted in the ground and allowed to grow, every daisy seed will produce a daisy and every parsnip seed a parsnip *and never once, by any, sort of accident* will the one produce the other. Nothing accidental could ever be so *positively* consistent.

The earth revolves around the sun at a distance of approximately ninety-three million miles. It has never varied in speed or distance in the long history of man's observation. Ten thousand other examples of the consistent behaviour of this universe surely rule out any possibility of "accident".

The alternative is that the whole universe was not only *designed* and *created*, but is still *maintained*. And the "Power" or "Thing" or "Person" who designed and still maintains the universe is what, for the want of a better word, we call *God*.

The second step is an assumption, but surely a very reasonable assumption, that the *one* who created *knows* what "He" has created. It does not follow, of course, that the thing created knows its creator. But let us see if we cannot go a step further. Man is a reasoning creature, able to make the statement: "I am" and to ask the question "Why am I?" This power of reasoning or "intelligence" must have come from the same source as the creature himself, since there is no other source.

Now it is a significant fact that, since the dawn of history, man has "felt" the existence of a Power or "Person" outside and above all life and creation. Whenever a new race of people have been discovered, they have always been found to have the same idea, long before they could have come under the influence of any other race. Only their interpretation of the idea differs. This seems to be a positive indication that God, being the only source of intelligence, *desires* man to recognise Him, and to seek to understand Him.

If we can make these assumptions we have already come a long way; in fact we stand upon the threshhold of a most important fact. When a man is faced with a problem — especially a mental problem — he will find no peace until he has found an acceptable solution. The following quotation from an old saint seems to fit the situation perfectly: "The soul is restless, till it finds its rest in Thee".

True peace of mind is dependent upon finding an answer to the conscious or unconscious question "What is God?" And this question is perhaps even more often expressed as "Where is God?" — a question which we tried to answer in chapter three. Nothing is more certain than that there is an answer, and that the answer can be found.

The science of psychology teaches us that when the human mind is faced with a serious problem, it very often tries to solve that problem by a process known as "rationalising", which is really "twisting the facts to suit the circumstances".

The Book of Genesis tries to teach us an inspired truth when it says that "God made man in His own image". This ought to be a valuable clue in seeking an answer to our problem about the nature of God. But the sad fact is, that man, right down the ages, has consistently "rationalised" by making God in the image of man.

As has been said earlier, most of our "rationalisings" about God have this one great weakness — that they put God at a distance. They put Him outside man and outside circumstance, and this would suggest that since God is infinite and man is finite, man can *never* really understand God.

If we could find one person who had solved this problem to his own complete satisfaction, and had proved the validity of his claim in a convincing manner, we would have the best possible start in our search. *Has there ever been such a person?*

We have the record of one such man, who not only publicly claimed that he and God were *one*, but who lived his short life in such a manner as to suggest that he spoke the simple truth. This was no megalomaniac with grandiose notions of his own importance, but on the contrary, a man renowned for His humility, truth and sincerity. Two thousand years of search and research by followers and opponents have never discredited this man, nor raised a valid doubt as to his sincerity. This man was Jesus, the son of a carpenter in a small and insignificant country known today as Palestine. It is obviously worthwhile studying what he had to say, not only of the nature of God, but of His accessibility to those who sincerely seek the truth.

Let us look, then, at what Jesus said about God. Perhaps the most significant thing He said was that God was our *Father*. In using this expression, He was, of course, establishing a relationship, and we should therefore first of all consider all the implications of this relationship.

Primarily, the Father is necessarily the origin of our existence. On even a purely human and material level this is accepted without question. Without a father we could not be. But humanity has also accepted without question that the father has an authority over his children, and expects a certain respect, and at least a measure of obedience. From the dawn of history, mankind has sensed that these things are *due* to the mysterious Being who, for want of a better title has been labelled "God". That is why man has sought, in many various ways, to "worship" God.

We could truthfully say that man has always conceded God's right to these things. But once we use the word *Father*, we change in a subtle way, the meaning of the words "respect" and "obedience". A person does not worship his father as a pagan worships his god. The adoration which he may feel is a fuller and a richer thing which, perhaps, only the term *love* can ever express. And even the obedience called for and rendered is something more than the blind, unreasoning, and often resentful service of a slave to his master. Beyond doubt Jesus desired to establish a sweeter, softer, and more acceptable relationship between man and God.

However, there is a vast difference between a father whom we can see, and a *Father* unseen, unknown and untouchable. Does Jesus clear up this difficulty? It is true that Jesus said "God is Spirit", and at first glance, this would appear to make the situation more difficult to comprehend, but fortunately He also said two other very significant things which throw light on the subject.

First of all, when teaching His disciples how to pray, He gave them a form of address to use: "Our Father, who art in heaven". It is unfortunate that this title has led many astray in the sense that they mentally "look upwards" when they pray. God seems to be at a distance.

But it must be understood that Jesus did not say "Our Father who who art in the *heavens* (a word indicating the sky or "space".) He said "in heaven". He used the same expression many times when speaking of "the kingdom" and in Luke 17 verse 20 made it quite clear that He was not speaking of any distant place by saying "the Kingdom of God is within you". Here is the clue: "Our Father is within".

The more we study this word "heaven" the more we become convinced that Jesus meant "the mind" or "the imagination". Our Father in heaven is not some figure dwelling in the immensities of space, but deep in the inner recesses of the mind.

It is when we add the second statement of Jesus that the full significance dawns upon us, for He said in John 14 verse 9: "He that hath seen me hath seen the Father". This does not mean that He Himself was claiming to be God, but merely that He was giving us a clear picture to carry in our minds when thinking of God. We must remember that *nothing* at all exists except as we see it in the mind, for the mind is the only means by which we can interpret the universe. We use the word "imagine" wisely, for it is the "image-in" the mind.

This takes us a mighty step forward, for now we have something visible and substantial to study. There is a touching little story told of a young boy whose father had found it necessary to travel to a distant part of the world. Missing the loved parent greatly, the boy stood one day before a full length portrait of his father and said wistfully: "I wish my father could step right out of the picture". This, in effect, is exactly what happened with the coming of Jesus on to the human scene — God "stepped right out of the picture" and became real to us.

Once this is realised and accepted, God ceases to be a mystery. He ceases to be out of reach and unapproachable. He becomes real and understandable.

Compare this new "image" — of a strong, tender, loving, understanding, forgiving *person* — with the dread image that has been in the minds of so many people for so many ages. The stern, unyielding, mysterious Power that broods over the universe, watching and criticising our every move; meting out punishments and storing up memories of our failures. The rigid and implacable standard against which our miserable lives will be measured and judged — a hopeless and impossible standard to which we, in our human frailty could never attain.

When the truth of all this breaks in upon our minds, we experience a great lifting of the spirit. Suddenly the impossible becomes possible; the strife ends, and a deep peace enters into the soul; the meaning of life becomes more clear. and a new sense of purpose takes hold of our lives.

If the true fulfilment of life — the true happiness — depends upon attaining a state of *harmony* with God, we can now approach the task of achieving that harmony without any conviction of reaching for the impossible. The prize is within our reach. Here is where the Apostle Paul had such a valuable word of advice for us. In Philippians 3 verses 13-14 he says: "Forgetting those things that are behind (the past) . . . and reaching forth to those things that lie in front, I press towards the mark for the prize . . ."

Throwing aside all the old memories and the misguided teachings; the influence of the past, with all its hoodoos and superstitions; and all our preconceived notions and ideas — in fact, "getting a new mind" — and then reaching forward, not to the unattainable, but to the *prize* that is within our reach.

24

What and How should we teach our Children?

To do justice to this most important subject we should start at the very beginning. Let us not forget that our responsibility does not begin when a child is born. It begins when a child is conceived. Incalculable harm is often done by parents because they overlook or do not realise this important fact.

So it must be stressed that young married people should be brought to a realisation that the nine months before a baby is born may well be the most important months of its life. It should never be forgotten that things said or done in the presence of the mother are in some strange way recorded in the unconscious entity which will one day be a human child.

Loud noises; any kind of quarrelling; unusual movements; shocks or emotional upheavals should be avoided like the plague. Both parents should make up their minds to conduct their whole lives at this time as if in the conscious presence of the child, setting the finest example of well ordered and disciplined living of which they are capable.

The best matched couple who ever lived would not always be in agreement upon every matter affecting their day-to-day living, but when disagreement becomes apparent they should be most careful to discuss matters quietly and reasonably, not allowing themselves to become excited or to raise their voices in emphasis. The ideal situation is for them to take such matters (where they concern important issues) *together* in prayer to God, for it is impossible to quarrel in His presence.

It is most important for the mother never to *brood* over the disagreements or disappointments of life. Not to allow these things to *worry* her, or to become despondent or resentful about them. It has been explained earlier in these notes, that the bodily secretions, the contents of the glands, take on chemical changes with changes of mood, and the unborn child can be a chief sufferer. It is not by accident that we have come to use such expressions as "I was bitter". Indeed bitter-

135

ness of mood is finally expressed in the "acid" content of the glands. When the mind is out of harmony, the bodily functions will not operate harmoniously, and the disorder or "dis-ease" may well be communicated first of all to the unborn child.

Peace, Love, Harmony, are essentials to be aimed at. Do all you can to achieve these things, and when you have done all that is within your power, hand over the rest to God in quiet trust and confidence.

The next step is also one which is frequently overlooked by parents and others. They vaguely imagine that for the first few months of its life, a baby is so unconscious of the world into which it has been born, that it cannot be greatly affected by what is going on around it. This is all the more dangerous because it is based upon a half truth.

The child is in a state of "unconscious" consciousness, not only for a few months, but for the first few years. But this does not mean that it is not affected by its environment. Indeed the reverse is the case. There is perhaps no time when a child is *more* susceptible to the influences with which it is surrounded. Every sound, sight or movement is recorded in its memory files for future reference. And when, at some later date, its built-in computor is called upon to give an answer to some demand, it is this recorded data that will help to shape the answer. Thus you will see how important it is for the parents to control, to the best of their ability, every detail of the environment with which the child is surrounded.

Let us mention two very important factors of which so many parents seem to be in ignorance. The first concerns the feeding of the young child. If the baby is breast fed, then the mood or state of mind of the mother is vitally important, for the content of the food will vary with the contentment of the mother. It has been known for a mother to be the "innocent" cause of her child having convulsions (sometimes leading to the death of the child) through feeding it while herself being consumed with rage, hatred or bitterness. This may be a rare and extreme case, but the fact remains that the mother feeds the child, not merely with milk, but with many other things which spring from her state of mind.

There are many mothers who, for one reason or another, are quite incapable of breast feeding their babies. God forgive those who can but *won't*. But those who genuinely cannot, often make the mistake which can have grave effects upon the child in after life. They assume that the food is all that matters to the child, and often will make a bottle of the best food which money can buy or that the doctor can advise, and then arrange to prop up the bottle in such a manner that the child can feed itself without further attention from the mother. This is a fatal mistake, as any good psychologist will tell you. The cradling arms of the mother; the proximity of the mother's body and the nearness of the face are as vitally important to the child as the contents of the bottle, and every wise mother will make every feed an act of *love* and *security*.

The second mistake is made by a vast number of parents quite innocently. It is that attitude of mind of parents which "lets well alone" when a child is happy and contented, but rushes to assist at the very first sign that something is amiss. Let us make the situation quite clear.

When a baby is born it is literally torn away from one environment which offers food and comfort and security automatically and without effort, and thrust into a new, strange and hostile environment in which it must learn to communicate before its needs can be met. Therefore, by the very nature of things, the first thing the child must learn to do is to draw attention to itself — otherwise it will not long continue to survive. Long before the baby can move any other parts of its body enough to attract attention, it learns to use its vocal chords. And one of the earliest lessons it learns is that the louder the noise it produces, the quicker will be the response.

This is sheer necessity in the early stages of the child's life, but it cannot be allowed to continue indefinitely or the parents' lives will be a misery. So training must start very soon, and it must be subtle. This is where so many parents make a bad error of judgement. When a child is quiet and apparently contented, they keep well away and "leave the child in peace". It does not occur to them that the child may enjoy their company and even their participation in its wriggling and chuckling.

On the other hand, if the child cries, they will rush at once to see what the trouble is. Thus a very early lesson which a child learns is "that it pays to be naughty" but "nobody is interested if you are good".

We are not suggesting for one moment that a child works out such a solution, or puts it even mentally into words. But the infallible computor built into its childish mind produces this answer from the data which has been fed into it.

A wise parent, then, will reward a child for being "good" by sharing in its contentment, but will be very wary of responding to every cry of distress. A cry does not always mean that the baby is in pain. It does not always mean that there is a pin sticking in somewhere, or a disturb-

ance of the stomach. The wise mother will soon learn the truth and
begin, from the earliest stages, to teach the child that a smile is more
powerful than a grimace, and that a chuckle is more fruitful than a
scream.

Let us now move on to the time when the child is able to talk and
take an interest in the things and people that make up its environment.
How soon can we begin to talk to these children of religion ?

Many earnest Christian people begin to teach their children about
God and about Jesus from a very early age. There are "Sunday Schools"
which admit children into what are called "baby classes" as early as
two or three years of age, and there must be few Christian children who
do not know the Name of Jesus before they are four years of age. Many
people believe that we cannot, indeed, begin too soon to teach the
children the basic "truths" of our religion.

It is impossible to lay down any hard and fast law upon this point
for the simple reason that it all depends upon the manner and content
of the teaching. A great deal of harm is done because children are
taught to *dread* the consequences of certain acts, and when the thoughts
of punishment are allied to the idea of God, a false foundation is laid
upon which it is very difficult at a later date to build a true idea of the
nature of God.

One thing should be said very clearly, and that is, that all negative
teaching is wrong in principle, and the earlier such teaching is given,
the more harm it can do. Fear is a bad companion for anybody, irres-
pective of age, and anything built upon a foundation of fear is bound to
be wrong in principle.

There are those who will promptly reply that the Bible tells us that
"the fear of God is the beginning of wisdom", but these people have
never understood the Scriptures. The word "fear" used in this connection has an entirely different meaning. A literal translation of the
Hebrew "Yirah" is not "fear" but "reverence" which is an entirely
different thing. It establishes a relationship much closer to that existing
between father and son than that between Lord and slave.

Putting all religion to one side for the moment, and regarding a
child as a mere biological specimen, there is an inborn belief that "those
things tending towards pleasure tend towards life", and "those things
tending towards pain, tend towards death", and since the first law of
nature is to survive, a promise of good will always be more effective
than a threat of evil. The young mind rejects and rebels (unconsciously
if not outwardly) against the type of teaching that threatens unpleasant

things, but it will grasp eagerly the type of teaching that is based upon the promise of joy or pleasure for its fulfilment.

Begin as early as you like to teach a child that all the joy and happiness of life that it may desire will come as a result, not of what others do, but of what they do for others. If they love others they will find love. If they make others happy they will find happiness. If they help others, they themselves will be helped. They should be taught that every good and lovely thing is associated with God, from Whom all goodness flows.

The Roman Catholics have a saying: "Give us your child until it is seven years old, and it will remain a good Catholic". There is probably a great deal of truth in this saying, but it is quoted only because it illustrates a very important fact about children. What they learn in the earliest years of their lives, will probably influence them for their whole lives. In fact, it is one of the great tragedies of life that most people cannot "un-learn" some of the things that they were taught as small children. For this reason we should be extremely careful what we teach our children.

The Sunday School has its rightful place in the social and religious life of all Christian people, yet more harm is done to the mental health of the nation by Sunday Schools than is commonly realised. This does not mean that we should do away with Sunday Schools, but it certainly means that we should pay a great deal of attention to the way in which such schools are run, and be very careful about what is taught in them. Far too many people believe that because a Sunday School is a Christian institution organised by the Christian Church, it can do nothing but good. This is absolutely *not true*.

Before a teacher is licenced to teach in our *day* schools, a certain standard of efficiency, education and ability is demanded, and these qualities come only as a result of careful study and devotion to the task of learning. Yet all too often, Sunday School teachers are accepted and used for no better reason than that they are *willing*.

Since they are not paid for their work, it is considered that the Church must not make too heavy demands upon them. There is also the undoubted fact that in many Churches there is such a shortage of able and willing people to do the work that none can be denied the opportunity who volunteer. Thus we have the situation that, in thousands of Sunday Schools, utterly unskilled and totally unsuitable "teachers" have charge of the religious education of children for no better reason than that they are prepared to give up a certain amount of their time "in God's service".

With all due respect to these well meaning and kindly people, *they are not necessarily doing God a service*, and they may well be doing incalculable harm quite innocently. The standard set for those who would teach the most important truths of life should not be lower but *higher* than the standard set for secular education. A great reformation is needed within the Church as far as the education of our children is concerned.

It may be argued that the Church will never be able to find enough people who are prepared to undergo the necessary training; that such training would involve months or even years of *full time study* which few could afford to give. Then, in all seriousness, we must answer that the same terms apply to them as apply to our ministers, *we have to pay them*. We shall be told, of course, that the Churches cannot afford to pay Sunday School teachers, and the only answer to that is, that *we cannot afford* to place the religious education of our children in unskilled hands.

Obviously such a reform would take years to put into effect, even if the Churches can be persuaded to accept it, and one must therefore ask the question: "Is there any alternative?"

There is one alternative, and this is almost as revolutionary, since it would involve a complete change in the type of teaching given to the children. However, it has much to recommend it, and therefore we give a brief outline for your examination and consideration.

The suggested scheme does not mean that "just anybody" would still be able to teach in our Sunday Schools, but it would make things easier inasmuch as the only specialised knowledge would be more easily acquired, and the only basic qualification of the teacher would be a sound character and *a genuine love of children*.

No direct religious teaching would be included in the syllabus, at least up to the age of twelve. The children would be taught *courtesy, kindness, consideration and love*. Only the most carefully selected passages of Scripture would be used, and these, not specifically dealing with theological or doctrinal subjects, but rather a wide variety of simple stories chosen for their bearing upon the subjects enumerated.

All the great religions of the world — Christianity, Buddhism, Taoism, Hinduism, Moslem — have as a basic concept: *"Do unto others as you would that they should do unto you"* and the world abounds with stories having neither denominational nor religious emphasis, which enunciate this grand principle. The vitally important thing for us to teach the children is the art of living together in harmony. Teach the children also to have thankful hearts, to recognise and love all lovely things, to be creative and never destructive, and a foundation will be laid upon which the children, when they are old enough to think for themselves, can build a true faith, unhampered by prejudice and superstition.

Of course this is not all, it is merely a pointer to the right direction. It would be impossible to do justice to this tremendous subject in such a book as this. Indeed, the subject is worthy of a book to itself. What has been here written is merely to *set you thinking*.